a dictionary of bharata natya

ORIENT LONGMAN

Bombay Calcutta Madras New Delhi

Bangalore Hyderabad Patna

a dictionary of bharata natya

U.S.KRISHNA RAO

A Dictionary of Bharata Natya

First Published 1980

Orient Longman Ltd.

Registered Office:

3/5 Asaf Ali Road, New Delhi 110 002

Other Offices:

Kamani Marg, Ballard Estate, Bombay 400 038
17 Chittaranjan Avenue, Calcutta 700 072
160 Anna Salai, Madras 600 002
1/24 Asaf Ali Road, New Delhi 110 002
80/1 Mahatma Gandhi Road, Bangalore 560 001
3-5-820, Hyderguda, Hyderabad 500 001
S. P. Verma Road, Patna 800 001

Printed at Kalakshetra Publications Press,
Thiruvanmiyur, Madras 600 041

Published by Usha Aroor, Orient Longman Ltd.,
160 Anna Salai, Madras 600 002

Title-page design: K. Damodar

Title-page photograph
students of Sree Bhar

KEY TO PRONUNCIATION AND ABBREVIATIONS

a	**as in**	***a*gain**
ā	**„**	**c*ā*rt**
ai	**„**	**n*i*ne**
au	**„**	***ou*t**
b	**„**	***b*it**
bh	**„**	***Bh*arata**
c	**„**	***ch*oose**
ch	**„**	**su*ch h*eight**
d	**„**	**coup *d'* etat**
dh	**„**	**Sin*dh***
ḍ	**„**	***d*og**
ḍh	**„**	**a*d h*oc**
e	**„**	**r*ai*n**
g	**„**	***g*et**
gh	**„**	**a*gh*ast**
i	**„**	***i*nk**
ī	**„**	**m*ee*k**
j	**„**	***Ju*dge**
jh	**„**	***Jh*elum; as above with an aspirant**
k	**„**	**cut**
kh	**„**	***Kh*artoum**
l	**„**	***l*amp**
ḷ	**„**	**a hard l sound**
m	**„**	***m*an**
n	**„**	**ca*n***
ṅ	**„**	**go*ng***
ñ	**„**	**si*ng*e**
ṇ	**„**	**a hard n sound**

PREFACE

When Orient Longman, Madras, requested me to write a dictionary of technical terms of Bharata Natya, I accepted the assignment with enthusiasm because it was one of my own dreams to arrange these terms of Bharata Natya systematically. I am sure most dancers will welcome this dictionary, as both students and teachers interested in the study and propagation of Bharata Natya will find it extremely useful.

I am deeply grateful to Shrimati Vidya Hydari for her invaluable help in reorganising the arrangement of items in the dictionary. I also thank Shri H. N. Dwarakanath for typing the handwritten manuscript. My wife Shrimati U. K. Chandrabhaga Devi assisted me in proofreading and corrections and my thanks are due to her without whose critical views this work would be incomplete.

The dictionary is for the benefit of all those interested in Bharata Natya. I have tried to standardise the terminology of Bharata Natya in so far as is possible in a dynamic art in which varying views emerge from time to time. My principal sources have been the *Natya Shastra* and the *Abhinaya Darpana*, but more recent books have also been taken into account. I welcome any constructive criticism and suggestions that will help to make this dictionary a tribute to the pristine beauty of Bharata Natya.

U. S. KRISHNA

o	as in	*o*pen
p	,,	*p*in
ph	,,	u*p h*ill
r	,,	*r*ight
ṛ	,,	K*ri*shna
s	,,	*s*it
ś	,,	*sh*oe
ṣ	,,	S*ch*ubert
t	,,	en*t*ree
th	,,	Ma*th*ura; as above with an aspirant
ṭ	,,	*t*ime
ṭh	,,	ou*t h*ouse
u	,,	b*oo*k
ū	,,	c*oo*l
v	,,	*v*ery
w	,,	*w*est
y	,,	*y*ellow

NS: *Natya Shastra*
AD: *Abhinaya Darpana*

A

Abhanga (*Abhaṅga*): Bhanga; body slightly bent, weight on one leg, the other leg relaxed near the first. Depicts Rama, repose etc.

Abhitapta (*Abhitapta*) [NS]: Drishti bheda expressing vyabhichari bhava. The eyelids are moved slightly to indicate distress, pain.

Abhinaya (*Abhinaya*): Sanskrit word, made up of the prefix 'abhi' meaning 'towards' and the root 'ni' meaning 'to carry', i.e., carrying an idea or a play towards the audience; acting in which bhava, rasa and gestures are used. See also *Chaturvidha Abhinaya.*

Abhinaya Darpana (*Abhinaya Darpaṇa*): A treatise of gestures and postures used in dance and drama, written by Nandikeshwara. One of the standard books on Bharata Natya.

Abhisarika Nayika (*Abhisārikā Nāyikā*): A woman who goes to meet her lover in spite of many obstacles. One of the ashta nayikas. See *Nayika.*

Abhugna (*Abhugṅa*) [NS]: Hridaya krama; chest is slightly bent and lowered, back held up, shoulders bent. Denotes hurry, despair, fainting, fear, sorrow, sickness, a broken heart, touching a cold object, rain, shame.

Achurita (*Achurita*) [NS]: See *Angahara.*

Adavu (*Aḍavū*): Fundamental dance unit used in nritta where hands, feet, head, eyes and other parts of the body move in a coordinated manner. Resemblances between some adavus and karanas lead to the postulation that adavus are based on karanas. To fulfil the conditions of anga shuddha (purity of movement), the four lakshanas of an adavu must be correctly performed. These are sthanaka (posture assumed at the beginning and end of the adavu), nritta hasta (hasta used in its performance), chari (movements of hands and feet), hasta kshetra (position of hands throughout its performance). Adavuṣ are variously classified by natyacharyas, the writer's classification being as follows: tattu, mettu, natu, kattu, egaru tattu, egaru mettu, egaru kattu, tattu mettu, muktaya, jaru, jati, tandava, mandi, arudi, mai, nade, bhramari, plavana, rangakramana, ekapada tandava.

ADBHUTA (*Adbhuta*) [NS]: Drishti bheda expressing adbhuta rasa; the eyelids are curved slightly at the end, eyeballs raised and eyes widened.

———RASA (—*Rasa*): Rasa of wonder; presiding deity—Brahma; sthayi bhava—vismaya; representative colour—yellow. Vibhavas—sight of heavenly bodies, achieving something great, entrance to a great mansion, palace or temple, illusory or magical arts. Anubhavas—opening the eyes wide, staring fixedly, horripilation, tears of joy, perspiration, joy, uttering words of approbation. Vyabhichari bhavas—weeping, paralysis, choked voice, horripilation, agitation, hurry, inactivity, etc.

ADDAMI (*Aḍḍami*): Movement of the head and neck from side to side, corresponding to the Parivahita shiro bheda and Sundari greeva bheda. This is one of the most important movements in all Indian classical dance and denotes the beginning of dance, affection, love, satisfaction, uttering praise to the deity etc.

ADDITA (*Aḍḍita* [NS]: Bhaumi chari, one Agratalasanchara foot is rubbed against the forepart or back of the other.

——— : Bhaumi Mandala; the right foot is moved in Udghatita, moved round, Syandita chari then left foot Shakatasya chari, right foot moved back in Apakranta and Syandita chari left in Addita, right in Apakranta, left in Bhramari and finally right in Syandita chari striking the ground violently.

ADHAMA NAYIKA (*Adhama Nāyikā*): A characterless, quarrelsome, jealous woman. See *Nayika*.

ADHARA KRAMA (*Adhara Krama*) [NS]: Movements of the lower lip; 6 of these—Kampana, Samudgaka, Sandashtaka, Viniguhana, Visarga, Vivartana.

ADHEERA NAYIKA (*Adhīra Nāyikā*): A nayika who uses harsh words towards her lover who is at fault. See *Nayika*.

ADHOGATA (*Adhogata*) [NS]: Shiro bheda where head is bent down denoting shame, bowing and sorrow.

ADHOMUKHA (*Adhomukha*) [AD]: Shiro bheda where head is bent to denote bashfulness, grief, bowing, anxiety, fainting, plunging into water.

ADHYARDHIKA (*Adhyardhika*) [NS]: Bhaumi chari. Left foot is placed on the heel of the right foot and the latter drawn away.

ADI TALA (*Ādi Tāla*): The most common tala in Karnatak music and Bharata Natya; Triputa tala in Chaturashra jati, having one laghu (4 counts) and two drutas (2 counts each). Represented thus $1_4 00$ and counted by clapping and counting on 3 fingers (4 counts) followed by a clap and a wave and another clap and wave (4 counts), totalling 8 counts. Also called Chaturashra-Triputa tala. See *Tala*.

AGRATALA SANCHARA (*Agratala Sañcāra*) [NS]: Pada krama; heels are raised, big toe is put forward and the other toes are bent. Used in sthanaka; denotes arguing, breaking, kicking, striking the ground, walking, throwing away something, walking on the forepart of the foot because of a wound.

AHARYABHINAYA (*Ahāryābhinaya*): Abhinaya through costume, make-up, jewellery etc. worn according to the character (patra) depicted. See *Chaturvidha Abhinaya*.

AINDRA STHANAKA (*Aindra Sthānaka*) [AD]: Sthanaka, one leg bent, the other leg and knee raised, hands hung down. Depicts Indra, a king.

AKAMPITA (*Akampita*) [NS]: Shiro bheda; head is moved up and down slowly denoting teaching, questioning, addressing, ordering.

AKASHA BHRAMARI (*Ākāśa Bhramari*) [AD]: Bhramari; feet are stretched wide apart in a jump and then the entire body is moved round.

AKASHIKI CHARI (*Ākāśiki Cāri*) [NS]: Chari or movement of one foot in the air, aerial chari. Sixteen of these—Akshipta, Alata, Apakranta, Aviddha, Bhramari, Bhujangatrasita, Dandapada,

Dolapada, Harinapluta, Nupurapadika, Parshvakranta, Suchi, Udvritta, Urdhvajanu, Vidyudbhranta.

AKASHIKI MANDALA (*Ākaśiki Maṇḍala*) [NS]: Aerial mandalas; 10 of these—Alata, Atikranta, Dandapada, Kranta, Lalita, Lalitasanchara, Suchividdha, Vamaviddha, Vichitra, Vihrata.

AKEKARA (*Ākekara*) [NS]: Drishti bheda expressing vyabhichari bhava; eyes are half shut, eyelids slightly contracted and eyeballs turned up.

AKSHARA KALA (*Akṣara Kāla*): A single time, measure, a unit.

AKSHIPTA (*Ākśipta*) [NS]: Akashiki chari. Kunchita foot is thrown up and placed quickly on an Anchita foot by crossing the shank of the other leg.

AKSHIPTAKA (*Ākśiptaka*) [NS]: See *Angahara.*

AKSHIPTARECHITA (*Ākśiptarecita*) [NS]: See *Angahara.*

——— [NS]: See *Karana.*

ALAGA (*Alaga*) [AD]: Utplavana; leaping with both feet, Shikhara hands on hip.

ALAMBANA VIBHAVA (*Ālambana Vibhāva*) [NS]: Main cause of bhava, i.e. the nayaka-nayika relationship etc. See *Vibhava.*

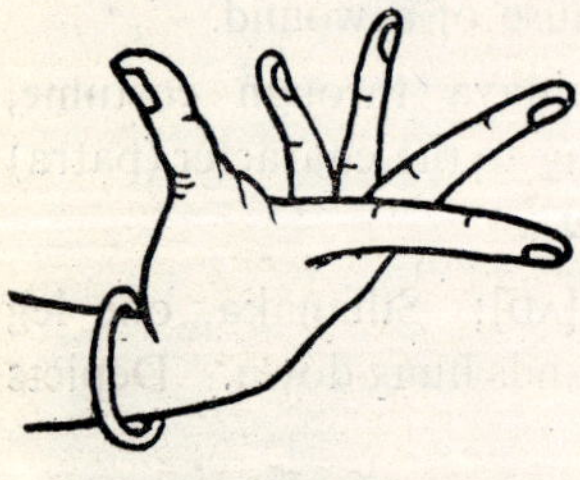

Alapadma

ALAPADMA (*Ālapadma*) [AD]: Asamyuta hasta; the fingers are opened and separated, little finger over palm, others sloping downward, thumb in line with palm. Denotes (AD) lotus, elephant, apple, circular movement, breasts, looking-glass, full moon, beauty, hair tied in a knot, moon, tower, village, height, mountain, cart, anger, etc. and (NS) prevention, a woman alluding to herself, asking 'who are you', saying 'nonsense', 'it is not so'.

ALAPALLAVA (*Ālapallava*) [NS]: Asamyuta hasta. See *Alapadma.*

ALARIPPU (*Alārippu*): Literally, 'blossoming forth'; an invocation dance performed at the beginning of every Bharata Natya recital, where through a series of pure nritta movements of the face and all parts of the body, the body is dedicated to

God. May be set to any of the five jatis and uses Solkattu syllables.

ALASYA (*Ālasya*) [NS]: Vyabhichari bhava of indolence; vibhavas— sickness, lassitude, pregnancy, satiety; anubhavas— lying or sitting down, aversion to work, drowsiness, sleep etc.

ALATA (*Ālāta*) [NS]: Akashiki chari; one foot is stretched back, placed in, and rested on its heel.

——— [NS]: Akashiki mandala; right foot is moved in Suchi chari, left in Apakranta chari and right in Parshvakranta and left in Alata chari; this is repeated six or seven times; then right foot is moved in Apakranta chari and left in Atikranta and Bhramari charis.

——— [NS]: See *Karana.*

ALATAKA (*Ālātaka*)[NS]: See *Angahara.*

ALIDHA (*Ālidha*) [NS]: See *Angahara.*

——— [AD]: Mandala; with left hand Shikhara, right Katakamukha, the left foot is placed one and a half cubits before the right.

——— [NS]: Sthanaka; right foot in Mandala sthanaka is drawn five talas away from the other.

ALOKITA (*Ālokita*) [AD]: Dhrishti bheda; glancing keenly and quickly with open eyes; denotes the turning of a potter's wheel, showing different things, begging.

ALOLITA (*Ālolita*) [AD]: Shiro bheda; the head is rolled round and round; denotes drowsiness, intoxication, fainting, laughing uproariously, travelling etc.

AMARSHA (*Amarṣa*) [NS]: Vyabhichari bhava of indignation; vibhavas —abuses or insults; anubhavas —shaking the head, perspiring, thinking, looking for ways and means of vengeance, looking for allies.

ANCHITA (*Añcita*) [NS]: Greeva bheda; the neck and head are turned back; denotes hanging, arranging hair, looking upwards.

——— [NS]: See *Karana.*

——— [NS]: Pada krama; heels are placed on the ground, forepart of the foot and toes raised denotes moving with a wound on the forefoot, turning in all directions, being struck by something; used in various bhramaris.

——— [NS]: Shiro bheda; head is bent slightly to one side; denotes sickness, swooning, intoxication, anxiety, sorrow.

ANGA (*Aṅga*): See *Angikabhinaya*.

ANGAHARA (*Aṅgahāra*) [NS]: Movement consisting of 4, 6, 7, 8 or 9 karanas. (2 karanas =1 matrika, 2, 3, or 4 matrikas=1 angahara.) Thirtytwo of these:

Acchurita: Nupura karana, turn the trika, do Vyamsita karana; turn the trika again and perform successively Alataka karana from the left and Suchi, Karihasta and Katicchinna karanas.

Ākshiptaka: Do successively Nupura, Vikshipta, Alataka, Akshipta, Uromandala, Nitamba, Karihasta and Katicchinna karanas.

Ākshiptarechita: Swastika feet in rechita, hands in Swastika, separate hands and with the same rechita movement, throw them up and perform Udvritta, Akshipta, Uromandala, Nitamba, Karihasta and Katicchinna karanas.

Alātaka: With hands in Swastika and Vyamsita perform Alataka, Urdhvajanu, Nikunchita, Ardhasuchi, Vikshipta, Udvritta, Akshipta, Karihasta and Katicchinna karanas.

Ālidha: In Vyamsita karana, hands on shoulders, do Nupura karana with left foot, Alata and Akshipta karanas with right, Uromandala gestures with hands; then perform Karihasta and Katicchinna karanas.

Aparājita: Assuming Dandapada karana hands in Vikshipta and Akshipta movement, Vyamsita karana is performed, the left hand moving along the left foot. Then with hands in Chaturashra and feet in Nikuttita, Bhujangatrasita karana is done. With hands in Udveshtita, successively Nikuttita, Akshipta, Uromandala, Karihasta and Katicchinna karanas are executed.

Apaviddha: Apaviddha and Suchividdha karanas are done using Udveshtita hand movements, then a trika turn, showing hands in Uromandala and Katicchinna karana is done.

Ardhanikuttaka: Nupurapadika is done swiftly, hands moving in harmony with the feet; then the trika turn and Nukuttita with hands and feet, followed by Uromandala, Karihasta, Katicchinna and Ardhanikuttaka karanas.

Bhramara: Nupurapada, Akshipta, Katicchinna, Suchividdha, Nitamba, Karihasta, Uromandala and Katicchinna karanas are performed in succession.

Gatimandala: Assuming Mandala sthanaka, the hands are moved in Rechita, feet in Udghatita, then the following karanas are performed successively—Mattali, Akshipta, Uromandala, Katicchinna.

Madavilāsita: Moving with Dola hands and Swastikapasrata feet, hands assume Anchita and Valita, and Talasamghattita, Nikuttita, Urudvritta, Karihasta and Katicchinna karanas are performed.

Mattakrīda: Nupura karana is performed by turning trika; Bhujangatrasita with right foot and then, Akshiptaka, Chinna, Bhramaraka, Uromandala, Nitamba, Karihasta and Katicchinna karanas.

Mattaskhalita: Mattali karana is performed; the right hand is moved round, bent and placed near the right cheek and then Apaviddha, Talasamsphotita, Karihasta and Katicchinna karanas are performed.

Parāvritta: Assuming Janita karana and putting one foot forward, the following are performed: Alataka karana, turning the trika in Bhramari chari, then placing left hand on cheek and doing Katicchinna karana.

Paricchinna: Assuming Samapada sthanaka the following karanas and charis are performed—Parichhinna karana, Bhramaraka chari with Aviddha right foot, Suchi karana with left, then Atikranta, Bhujangatrasita, Karihasta and Katicchinna karanas.

Parivrittakarechita: With hands held loose in Swastika over the head, body bent, and Rechita with left hand; body straightened, and Rechita repeated, hands changed to Lata; and Vrischika, Rechita, Karihasta, Bhujangatrasita and Akshipta karanas performed in succession.

Pārshvaccheda: Holding Nikuttita hands at the chest, Urdhvajanu, Akshipta, Swastika karanas are performed, trika turned round and Uromandala, Nitamba, Karihasta and Katicchinna karanas performed.

Pārshvaswastika: Swastika is assumed and Ardhanikuttaka done on one side; repeated the other side; then with Vyavartita hand kept on thigh, Urudvritta, Akshipta, Nitamba, Karihasta and Katicchinna karanas are preformed.

Paryāshtaka: Talapushpaputa, Apaviddha and Vartita karanas are done; then assuming Pratyalidha sthanaka, Nikuttita, Urudvritta, Akshipta, Uromandala, Nitamba, Karihasta and Katicchinna karanas are performed.

Rechita: Rechita hand is shown bent to one side with Rechita movement, then repeated, bending the body and Nupurapada, Bhujangatrasita, Rechita, Uromandala and Katicchinna karanas performed.

Sambhrānta: In Vikshipta karana the left hand thrown out in Suchi, right hand placed on chest and trika round turned in Bhramari chari; then Nupurapada, Akshipta, Ardhaswastika, Nitamba, Karihasta, Uromandala and Katicchinna karanas are performed.

Sthirahasta: Assuming Samapada sthanaka, the arms are stretched out and thrown up with the left hand above the shoulders; then assuming Pratyalidha sthanaka, the following karanas are performed—Nikuttita, Urudvritta, Akshipta, Swastika, Nitamba, Karihasta and Katicchinna.

Sūchividdha: Hands are held in Alapallava and Suchimukha and the following karanas are performed—Vikshipta, Avartita, Nikuttita, Urudvritta, Akshipta, Uromandala, Karihasta and Katicchinna.

Swastikarechita: With hands and feet in Rechita, Vrischika karana is performed; then with hands and feet as before, Nikuttita karana and Lata hasta alternately with left hand and right hand are performed; lastly, Katicchinna karana is done.

Udghattita: Hands are moved in Udveshtita and Apaviddha, feet in Nikuttita, then hands changed to Uromandala and the following karanas are performed—Nitamba, Karihasta and Katicchinna.

Udvrittaka: Assuming Nupurapada chari, hands hung down at the sides, the following karanas are performed—Vikshipta, Suchi (with hands), then the trika is turned and Lata and Katicchinna karanas done.

Upasarpita: Apakranta chari and Vyamsita karana are performed with hands moving in Udveshita followed by Ardhasuchi, Vikshipta, Katicchinna, Udvritta, Akshipta, Karihasta and Katicchinna karanas.

Vaishakharechita: Rechita is performed with hands and body, repeating the body movement; with the body bent, Nupurapada chari and Bhujangatrasita, Rechita and Mandala-swastika karanas, then bending the shoulder Urudvritta, Akshipta, Uromandala, Karihasta and Katicchinna karanas are done.

Vidyudbhrānta: Suchi karana is assumed with left foot and Vidyudbhranta with right; they are then reversed and followed by Chinna karana, trika turn and Lata and Katicchinna karanas.

Vishkambha: With hands in Udveshtita and feet in Nikuttita, Urudvritta karana is performed changing hands to Chaturashra, feet remaining in Nikuttita. The following karanas are then performed—Bhujangatrasita (with hands in Udveshtita), Chinna, Bhramaraka (moving the trika), Karihasta and Katicchinna.

Vishkambhapasrita: Kuttita and Bhujangatrasita karanas are performed with Pataka hands in Rechita followed by Akshipta, Uromandala, Lata and Katicchinna karanas.

Vrishchikapasrita: Vrishchika karana is performed with Lata hands on the nose; the hands are then moved in Udveshtita and Nitamba and Karihasta and Katicchinna karanas are performed.

ANGIKABHINAYA (*Aṅgikābhinaya*) [AD, NS]: Abhinaya by moving parts of the body, viz., sharira (limbs), mukhaja (face) and chestakrita (entire body) or involving the angas (head, hands, chest, sides, waist or hips, feet), the pratyangas (the six other parts of the body—shoulder blades, arms, back, belly, thigh and calves, and shanks) and the upangas (the 12 parts of the head—eyes, eyebrows, eyeballs, cheeks, nose, jaw, lips, teeth, tongue, chin, face, shoulders). NS mentions only six upangas—eyes, eyebrows, nose, lips, cheeks, chin. See also *Chaturvidha-Abhinaya.*

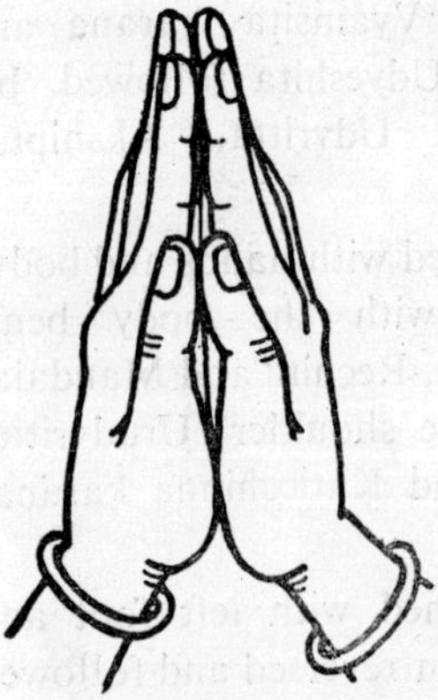

Anjali

ANJALI (*Añjali*) [AD, NS]: Samyuta hasta; two Pataka hands joined palm to palm, denotes salutation.

ANUBHAVA (*Anubhāva*) [NS]: Consequents of a bhava. See *Bhava.*

ANUDHA NAYIKA (*Anūdha Nāyikā*): Unmarried girl. See *Nayika.*

ANUDRUTA (*Anudtruta*): One Akshara Kala, or unit of time; denoted by a single clap. See *Tala.*

ANUGRAHA (*Anugraha*): Panchakriya of Nataraja; salvation as represented by the raised left big toe of the Nadanta pose. See *Nadanta.*

ANUKULA NAYAKA (*Anukūla Nāyakā*): A model husband who is faithful and clever. See *Nayaka.*

ANUPALLAVI (*Anupallavi*): Line following pallavi in a musical composition. See *Pallavi.*

ANUVRITTA (*Anuvṛtta*) [AD]: Drishti bheda; glancing quickly up and down; denotes angry looks, greeting friends.

APAHASITA (*Apahāsita*): An aspect of hasya rasa. Vulgar laughter, with tears in the eyes, and head and shoulders shaken violently.

APAKRANTA (*Apakrānta*) [NS]: Akashiki chari; with thighs in Valana, one Kunchita foot is raised and thrown down sideways.

——— [NS]: See *Karana.*

APARAJITA (*Aparājita*) [NS]: See *Angahara.*

APASMARA (*Apasmāra*) [NS]: Vyabhichari bhava of epilepsy; vibhavas—being possessed by an outside agency, a vision or memory of such beings, eating stale food, deserted houses, derangement of humours; anubhavas—trembling, throbbing, running, falling down, perspiring, foaming at the mouth, hiccoughing, licking the lips etc.

——— [NS]: Muyalaga; demon symbolising evil trampled down by Nataraja. See *Nadanta.*

APASRITA (*Apasrita*) [NS]: Parshva krama: Restore the side to normal position from the Vivartita movement. Denotes returning.

APASYANDITA (*Apasyandita*) [NS]: Bhaumi chari; place one foot and five talas away from the other.

APAVIDDHA (*Apaviddha*) [NS]: See *Karana.*

ARALA (*Arāḷa*) [AD, NS]: Asamyuta hasta; the forefinger of Pataka is curved in. Denotes (AD) drinking poison or nectar, water, strong wind; (NS) courage, pride, prowess, beauty, contentment, heavenly objects, poise, act of blessing, a woman gathering up or letting down her hair, preliminaries to a marriage, marital union, circumambulation, round objects, a crowd of men, calling someone, asking someone not to come in, uprooting something, wiping off sweat, enjoying a fragrant smell, abuse, saying 'too many things'.

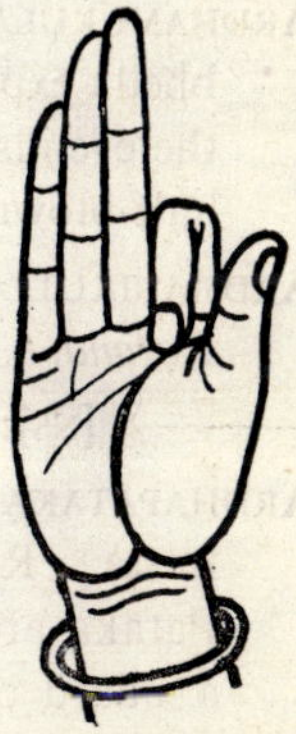

Arala

ARALAKATAKAMUKHA (*Arāḷakaṭakāmukha*) [NS]: Nritta hasta; two Alapallava hands turned upwards are changed to Padmakosha.

ARANGETRAM (*Araṅgeṭram*): Maiden performance, when, for the first time bells are tied to the feet. Usually takes place on an auspicious day in the presence of critics, artistes and well-wishers, after the dancer has acquired a sizeable repertoire of dance items. After the customary obeisance to God, guru and audience, the performance takes place and the guru is honoured with guru dakshina. Also called Rangapravesha.

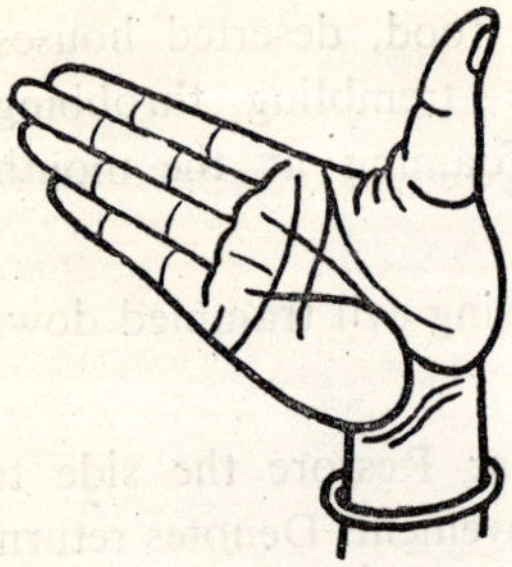

Ardhachandra

ARDHACHANDRA (*Ardhacandra*) [AD, NS]: Asamyuta hasta; thumb in Pataka is stretched out. Denotes (AD) phases of the moon, hand seizing the throat, spear, consecrating an image, a plate, origin, waist, musing oneself, meditation, prayers, touching the limbs, greetings by common people; and (NS) young trees, crescent moon, conch, jar, bracelet, to open something forcibly, exertion, thinness, drinking, a woman's waist, girdle, hip, face, ear-ring.

ARDHAMATTALI (*Ardhamattali*) [NS]: See *Karana*.

ARDHAMUKULA (*Ardhamukula*) [NS]: Drishti bheda expressing vyabhichari bhava of joy; the eyelids are half-opened, the eyeballs half-blown and mobile.

ARDHANIKUTTAKA (*Ardhanikuṭṭaka*) [NS]: See *Karana*.

———— [NS]: See *Angahara*.

ARDHAPATAKA (*Ardhapatāka*) [AD]: Asamyuta hasta. Ring finger and little finger of Pataka are bent in. Denotes (AD) leaves, a board or slab for writing or painting, bank of a river, saying both, knife, banner, tower.

Ardhapataka

ARDHARECHITA (*Ardharecita*) [NS]: See *Karana*.

———— [NS]: Nritta hasta; left hand Chaturashra, right, Rechita.

ARDHASUCHI (*Ardhasūci*) [AD]: One of the extra asamyuta hastas mentioned in AD. The forefinger in Kapittha is raised: denotes a sprout, young ones of a bird, big worms.

———— [NS]: See *Karana*.

ARDHASWASTIKA (*Ardhaswastika*) [NS]: See *Karana*.

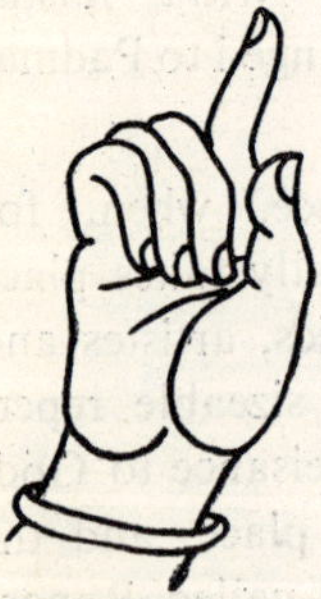

Ardhasuchi

ARUDI (*Aruḍi*): Adavu: rhythmic pattern performed by stamping the feet or doing muktaya adavus; generally done in a varnam or tillana, occasionally in padams; is performed from the first to the fifth (or vice-versa) beats of Adi tala etc.

ASAMYUTA HASTA (*Asamyuṭa Hasta*) [AD, NS]: Representative gestures using one hand only. AD mentions 28: Alapadma, Arala, Ardhachandra, Ardhapataka, Bhramara, Chandrakala, Chatura, Hamsapaksha, Hamsasya, Kangula, Kapittha, Kartarimukha, Katakamukha, Mayura, Mrigashirsha, Mukula, Mushti, Padmakosha, Pataka, Samdamsha, Sarpashirsha, Shikhara, Shukatunda, Simhamukha, Suchi, Tamrachuda, Tripataka, Trishula; 4 extra hastas, Ardhasuchi, Kataka, Palli, Vyaghra. NS Mentions 24: Alapallava (or Alapadma), Arala, Ardhachandra, Bhramara, Chatura, Hamsapaksha, Hamsasya, Kangula, Kapittha, Kartarimukha, Katakamukha, Mrigashirsha, Mukula, Mushti, Padmakosha, Pataka, Samdamsha, Sarpashirsha, Shikhara, Shukatunda, Suchimukha, Tamrachuda, Tripataka, Urnanabha.

ASHTA NAYIKA (*Aṣṭa Nāyikā*): Classification of heroines into eight types, viz., Abhisarika, Kalahantarita, Khandita, Proshitabhartrika, Swadheenabhartrika, Vasakasajjita, Vipralabdha, Virahotkhantita. See *Nayika*.

ASHTAPADI (*Aṣṭapadī*): Set of eight stanzas or verses; generally refers to verses of the *Geeta Govinda* by Jayadeva. See *Geeta Govinda*.

ASHVA (*Aśva*) [AD]: Utplavana; leaping with both feet, feet held together, hands in Tripataka.

ASKANDITA (*Askandita*) [NS]: Bhaumi mandala; right foot moved in Bhramari chari, left in Addita and Bhramari charis; then right in Urudvritta chari, left in Apakranta and Bhramari charis; left foot in Syandita and Shakatasya charis and stamped hard.

ASRA (*Aśra*) [NS]: Satvika bhava of weeping; vibhavas—excessive joy, fear, sorrow, indignation, smoke or collyrium hurting the eyes, yawning, staring, cold, illness.

ASUYA (*Asūya*) [NS]: Vyabhichari bhava of envy; vibhavas—other people's wealth or good fortune, intelligence, proficiency at sports, learning etc., offences, hatred; anubhavas—finding fault with others, decrying their virtues, not giving them credit, downcast face, knitting the brows, abusing others publicly.

ATIBHANGA (*Atibhaṅga*): Bhanga; one leg bent back (or forward), the other bent at the knee. Depicts tandava aspect, shooting arrows, throwing missiles.

ATIHASITA (*Atihasita*) [NS]: An aspect of hasya rasa. Excessive laughter; shown by expanded eyes and face, loud laughter, holding sides with hands.

ATIKRANTA (*Atikrānta*) [NS]: Akashiki chari; lift up a Kunchita foot, move it forward and place on the ground.

——— [NS]: Akashiki mandala; move right foot in Janita chari and Shakatasya chari, left foot in Alata and right in Parshvakranta charis; left in Suchi and right in Apakranta chari; again left in Suchi and Bhramari chari by turning the trika; right foot in Udvritta, left in Alata charis; change left foot to Bhramari chari, then to Alata chari, and right to Dandapada chari.

——— [NS]: See *Karana*.

ATTA TALA (*Aṭṭa Tāla*): Tala having 2 laghus and 2 drutas; generally 2 khanda laghus and 2 drutas, thus, 5+5+2+2, totalling 14 matras. See *Tala*.

AUTSUKYA (*Autsukya*) [NS]: Vyabhichari bhava of impatience; vibhavas—separation from loved ones, remembering them, the sight of a garden etc.; anubhavas—sighing, thinking with downcast face, sleepiness, desire to lie down, etc.

AVADHUTA (*Avadhūta*) [NS]: Shiro bheda; the head is turned down once; denotes giving a message, invoking a deity, conversation, beckoning etc.

AVAHITTA (*Avahitta*) [AD]: Samyuta hasta; two Alapadma hands, palms facing upwards are held at the chest. Denotes catching a ball, breasts, shringara rasa.

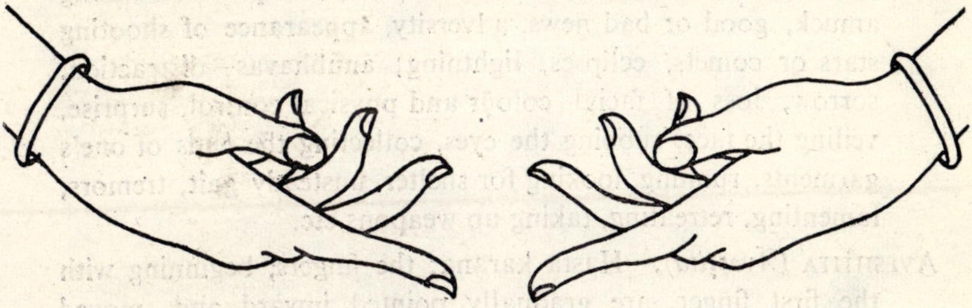

Avahitta (*AD*)

——— [NS]: Samyuta hasta; two Shukatunda hands meet at chest, are bent and lowered; denotes weakness, a sign, showing one's body, thinness of the body, longing for the beloved.

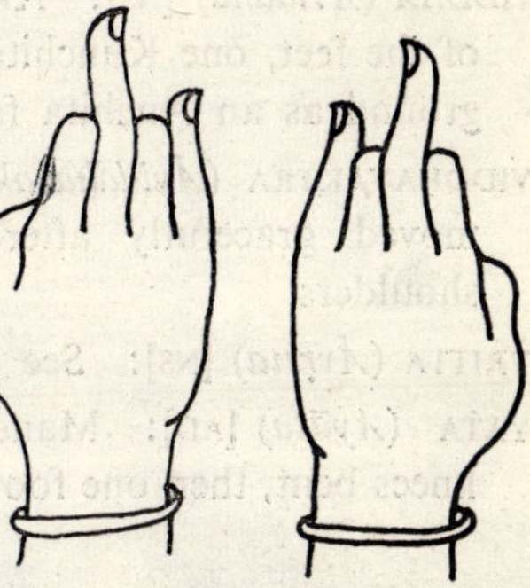

Avahitta (*NS*)

——— [NS]: Vyabhichari bhava of dissimulation ; vibhavas—shame, fear, defeat, respect, deceit; anubhavas—another person, looking downwards, break in speech, feigned patience, etc.

AVAHITTAKA (*Avahittaka*) [NS]: See *Karana*.

AVALOKITA (*Avalokita*) [AD]: Drishti bheda; looking down with the eyes. Denotes a shadow, reflection, exercise, fatigue, study, looking at one's limbs.

AVANADDHA (*Avanaddha*): Musical instruments covered with skin such as mridangam, etc. See *Sangeeta Vadya*.

AVARTA (*Āvarta*) [NS]: Bhaumi madala; right foot moved in Janita chari, left in Talasanchara chari, right Shakatasya and Urudvritta charis, left Apakranta chari, turning backward and then Chashagata chari, right in Skandita chari, left, Shakatasya chari, right, Bharamari chari turning the trika round, left foot in Apakranta chari.

AVARTITA (*Āvartita*) [NS]: Jangha Krama; left foot turned to the right, and vice versa; denotes a jester's way of walking.

AVEGA (*Āvega*) [NS]: Vyabhichari bhava of agitation; vibhavas—portents, wind or rain, outbreak of fire, elephants running amuck, good or bad news, adversity, appearance of shooting stars or comets, eclipses, lightning; anubhavas—distraction, sorrow, loss of facial colour and physical control, surprise, veiling the face, rubbing the eyes, collecting the ends of one's garments, running, looking for shelter, unsteady gait, tremors, lamenting, retreating, taking up weapons etc.

AVESHTITA (*Āveṣṭita*): Hasta karana; the fingers, beginning with the first finger, are gradually pointed inward and moved round.

AVIDDHA (*Āviddha*) [NS]: Akashiki chari, from Swastika position of the feet, one Kunchita foot is stretched and placed on the ground as an Anchita foot.

AVIDDHAVAKTRA (*Āviddhavaktra*) [NS]: Nritta hasta; two hands moved gracefully after successively touching the opposite shoulders.

AVRITTA (*Āvṛtta*) [NS]: See *Karana*.

AYATA (*Ayāta*) [AD]: Mandala; feet placed one cubit apart, knees bent, then one foot placed on the knee of the other leg.

B

BADDHA (*Baddha*) [NS]: Bhaumi chari; shanks are crossed and thighs are moved sideways.

BANDHAVYA HASTA (*Bāndhavya Hasta*) [AD]: Hasta depicting a relationship. Thus: *Husband and wife*: Left hand Shikhara, right hand Mrigashirsha. *Mother*: Left hand Ardhachandra near the belly, right hand Samdamsha and changed to Mrigashirsha over left hand. *Daughter*: As for *Mother*. *Father*: Left hand Ardhachandra at the belly and right Samdamsha, changed to Shikhara over left hand. *Son*: As for *Father*. *Mother-in-law*: Right hand Hamsasya at throat and left Samdamsha near it; the left hand is then rubbed over the belly. *Father-in-law*: As for *Mother-in-law* but with right hand Shikhara. *Elder/younger brother*: Mayura hands moved from sides to front denotes elder brother; Mayura hands moved from front to sides denotes younger brother. *Husband's brother:* Left hand Shikhara, right Kartarimukha placed at either side.

BHANGA (*Bhaṅga*): Posture. These are four in number. Abhanga, Atibhanga, Samabhanga, Tribhanga.

BHARATA (*Bharata*): The author, Bharata Muni, of *Natya Sastra*. Another connotation: 'Bha' stands for bhava, 'ra' for raga, 'ta' for tala, hence Bharata Natya is that natya which has bhava, raga and tala. Sanskrit literature contains reference to other Bharatas—the brothers of Rama and Bahubali, Shakuntala's son, etc.

BHARATARNAVA (*Bharatārṇava*): Treatise on dance by Nandikeshwara.

BHAUMI CHARI (*Bhaumi Cāri*) [NS]: 'Earthy' charis; charis performed with one foot on the ground; 16 of these—Addita, Adhyardhika, Apasyandita, Baddha, Chashagati, Edakakridita, Janita, Mattali, Samapada, Samosaritamattali, Shakatasya, Sthitavarta, Syandita, Urudvritta, Utsyandita, Vichyava.

BHAUMI MANDALA (*Bhaumi Maṇḍala*) [NS]: 'Earthy' mandalas; mandalas or combinations of charis performed with feet on the ground; 10 of these—Addita, Adhyardha, Askandita, Avarta, Bhramara, Chashagata, Edakakridita, Pishtakutta, Samosarita, Shakatasya.

BHAVA (*Bhāva*) [NS]: State of mind; cause or instrument of a rasa, sentiment. Bhava is depicted through words, gestures, and representation of the temperament. The word is derived from the Sanskrit 'bhavayanti'—to pervade or infuse. Any bhava has both *vibhavas* (determinants) and *anubhavas* (consequents). NS mentions sthayi, vyabhichari and satvika bhavas or dominant, transitory and temperamental states.

BHAYA (*Bhaya*) [NS]: Sthayi bhava of fear; gives rise to bhayanaka rasa; vibhavas—offending superiors, journeying through a forest, seeing or hearing wild animals, owls etc., a dark night, a deserted house; anubhavas—trembling, licking the lips, dryness of the mouth, running away, etc.

BHAYANAKA (*Bhayānaka*) [NS]: Drishti bheda expressing bhayanaka rasa; the eyelids are drawn up and fixed, the eyeball gleaming, turned up and fearful.

——— RASA (*—Rasa*): Sentiment of fear; presiding deity, Yamakala; sthayi bhava, bhaya (fear); representative colour, black; vibhavas—terrible noises, ghosts, panic, anxiety, etc.; anubhavas—trembling of hands and feet, horripilation, trembling, fear, stupefaction, dejection, agitation, change of colour, loss of voice; vyabhichari bhavas—paralysis, perspiration, choked voice, horripilation, trembling, fear, stupefaction, dejection, agitation, restlessness, epilepsy, death.

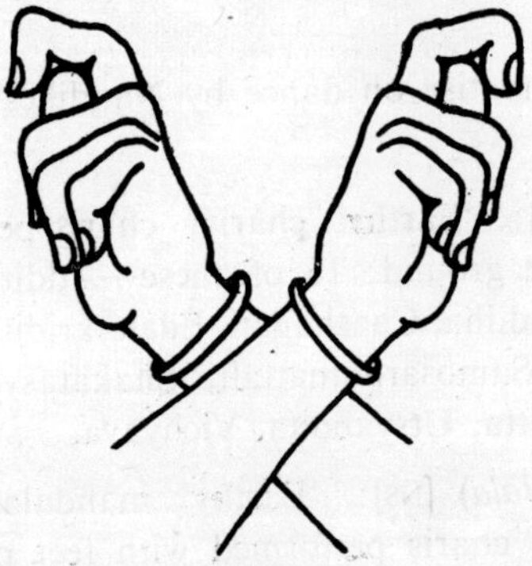

Bherunda

BHERUNDA (*Bhēruṇḍa*) [AD]: Samyuta hasta; two Kapittha hands are joined at the wrists, palms facing each other or away from each other; denotes bherunda, a pair of birds.

BHRAMANA (*Bhramaṇa*) [NS]: Tara bheda; eyeballs are turned round at random. Depicts veera and raudra rasa.

BHRAMARA (*Bhràmara*) [NS]: See *Angahara*.

——— [AD, NS]: Asamyuta hasta; lit. 'the bee'; the thumb and middle finger touch in a curve, the forefinger is curved in and the remaining fingers separated and stretched out. Denotes (AD) a bee, a parrot, a wing, a crane, a cuckoo, various birds; (NS) plucking flowers, ear-ring, a rebuke, pride in one's power, quickness, beating time etc.

——— [NS]: Bhaumi mandala; right foot in Janita chari, left in Syandita chari, right in Shakatasya and left foot is stretched; right is then moved in

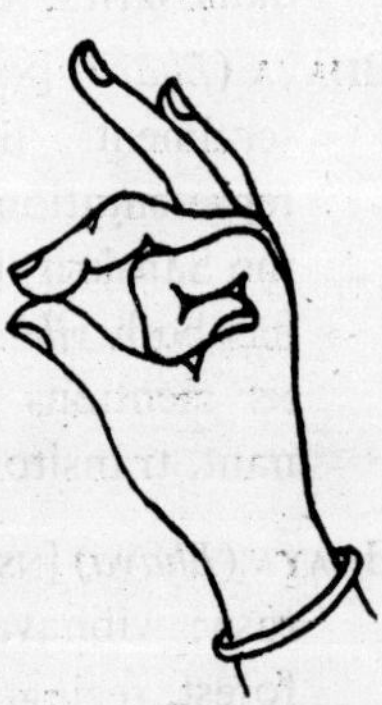

Bhramara

Bhramari chari turning the trika, left in Syandita chari, right in Shakatasya, finally left in Atikranta and Bhramari charis by turning round.

BHRAMARAKA (*Bhramaraka*) [NS]: See *Karana*.

BHRAMARI (*Bhramarī*) [AD]: Circling movements; ways of describing a circle; seven of these—Akasha, Anga, Chakra, Ekapada, Garuda, Kunchita, Utpluta.

——— [AD]: Adavu; turning round on one foot or walking round.

——— [NS]: Akashiki chari; the foot in Atikranta chari is thrown up and the entire body turned round. Then the second foot is turned on the sole.

BHRUCHALANA (*Brūcalana*) [NS]: Movement of the eyebrows; seven of these—Bhrukuti, Chatura, Kunchita, Patana, Rechita, Sahaja, Utkshepa.

BHRUKUTI (*Bhṛkuṭī*) [NS]: Bhru chalana; knitted brows; the roots of the eyebrows are raised. Denotes anger, a dazzling light.

BHUGNA (*Bhugna*) [NS]: Mukha bheda; slightly open mouth. Depicts shame, discouragement, impatience, anxiety, discipline, consultation, natural position for ascetics.

BHUJANGA GATI (*Bhujaṅga Gati*) [AD]: Gati bheda of the snake. Standing on toes and jumping forward holding Tripataka hands at either side.

BHUJANGANCHITA (*Bhujaṅgañcita*) [NS]: See *Karana*.

BHUNJANGATRASITA (*Bhunjaṅgatrāṣita*) [NS]: Akashiki chari; one Kunchita foot is thrown up and the waist, knee and thigh of the other leg are turned round.

——— [NS]: See *Karana*.

BHUJANGATRASTARECHITA (*Bhujaṅgatrāstarecita*) [NS]: See *Karana*.

BIBHATSA (*Bībhatsa*) [NS]: Drishti bheda expressing bibhatsa rasa or disgust; corners of the eyes nearly cover the eyelids; eyeballs shaken, eyelashes held still and close to each other.

———RASA (*—Rasa*) [NS]: Sentiment of disgust; odiousness; presiding deity, Shiva; sthayi bhava, jugupsa; representative colour, blue; vibhavas—hearing unpleasant things, seeing or discussing offensive, impure or harmful things; anubhavas—

inactivity, narrowing of the mouth, vomiting, spitting, shaking of the limbs etc.; vyabhichari bhavas—epilepsy, fainting, sickness, death etc.

BRAHMA (*Brahma*) [AD]: Sthanaka; sitting in padmasana pose; denotes meditation etc.

C

CHAKRA (*Cakra*) [AD]: Bhramari; moving round rapidly with feet on ground, hands in Tripataka.

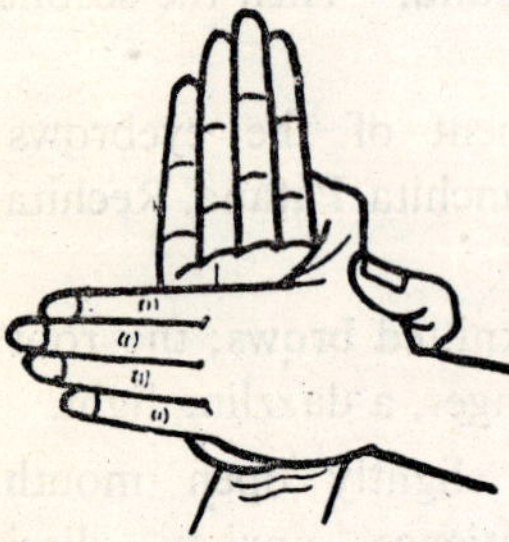

Chakra

—— [AD]: Samyuta hasta; the palms of Ardhachandra hands are put across each other, facing each other and at right angles. Denotes a wheel.

CHAKRA MANDALA (*Cakra Maṇḍala*) [NS]: See *Karana*.

CHALANA (*Calana*) [AD]: Chari; the foot is moved forward, as in walking.

—— [NS]: Tara bheda; eyeballs are trembled; used in depicting bhayanaka rasa.

CHANDRAKALA (*Candrakalā*) [AD]: Asamyuta hasta; the thumb in Suchi is stretched away from the palm. Denotes the moon, the face, span of the thumb and index finger, objects of the shape the hasta takes, Shiva's crescent moon, Ganga, a cudgel.

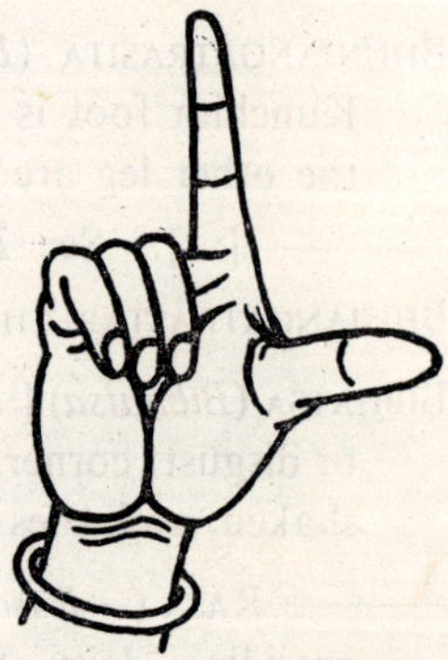

Chandrakala

CHANKRAMANA (*Cankramana*) (*Cāri*) [AD]: Raising the feet alternately sideways and jumping to sides.

CHAPALATA (*Capalata*) [NS]: Vyabhichari bhava of inconstancy; vibhavas—love, hatred, malice, impatience, jealousy, opposition; anubhavas—harsh words, rebuke, breathing hard, killing someone, taking someone prisoner, goading etc.

CHAPU TALA (*Cāpu Tāla*): Tala indicated by clapping (chapu) according to the fundamental rhythm; thus Mishra Chapu means clapping three times in mishra rhythm, Khanda Chapu, clapping three times in khanda rhythm.

CHARANA (*Caraṇa*): Third part of the musical sequence following pallavi and anupallavi.

CHARI (*Cāri*) [AD, NS]: Movements of one foot; AD mentions eight of these—Chalana, Chankramana, Kuttana, Lolita, Luthita, Sarana, Vegini, Vishama. NS mentions 2 kinds: See *Akashiki Chari, Bhaumi Chari.*

CHASHAGATA (*Cāśagata*) [NS]: Bhaumi mandala; going round with feet in Chasagati chari; used in depicting personal combat, fighting a duel.

CHASHAGATI (*Cāśagati*) [NS]: Bhaumi chari; right foot put forward and drawn back, simultaneously left foot drawn back and put forward.

CHATURA (*Catura*) [AD]: Bhru chalana; the eyebrows are moved slightly and extended in a pleasing manner. Denotes love, sportiveness, something that pleases, pleasant sensation, awakening.

——— [AD]: Asamyuta hasta; thumb placed at base of third finger, first, second and third fingers joined and stretched out, little finger separated and stretched out. Denotes musk, a small amount, gold, copper, iron, an eye, wet, sorrow, aesthetic pleasure, difference of castes, proof, sweetness, slow gait, breaking something to pieces, face, oil, ghee.

Chatura

——— [NS]: See *Karana.*

CHATURASHRA (*Caturaśra*): In Vaishnava sthanaka, the hands are moved about the waist and navel with the chest raised.

——— [NS]: Nritta hasta: both hands Katakamukha held at the chest.

———JATI (——*Jāti*): Laghu of 4 counts also called Chatushra jati. See *Tala*.

CHATURVIDHA ABHINAYA (*Caturvidha Abhinaya*) [AD, NS]: Four kinds of abhinaya, viz., aharyabhinaya, angikabhinaya, satvikabhinaya, vachikabhinaya.

CHESHTAKRITA (*Ceṣṭakrita*) [AD, NS]: See *Angikabhinaya.*

CHIBUKA KRAMA (*Cibuka Krama*) [NS]: Chin movements; seven in number—Chinna, Chikita or Chuksita, Dashta, Khandana, Kuttana, Lehita, Sama.

CHIKITA (*Cikita*) [NS]: Chibuka krama; See CHUKSITA.

CHINNA (*Chinna*) [NS]: Chibuka krama; lips meet each other and are held close. Denotes sickness, fear, cold, taking exercise, looking angrily.

———— [NS]: See *Karana*.

———— [NS]: Kati krama; the middle of the waist is turned. Denotes exercising, hurry and looking around.

CHINTA (*Cintā*) [NS]: Vyabhichari bhava of anxiety; vibhavas—loss of wealth, theft of a favourite object, poverty; anubhavas—breathing deeply, sighing, showing agony, meditating, thinking with downcast face, growing thin, etc.

CHUKSITA (*Cuksita*) [NS]: Chibuka krama; lips are held wide apart; denotes yawning; also called *Chikita*.

D

DAINYA (*Dainya*) [NS]: Vyabhichari bhava of depression. Vibhavas—poverty, mental agony, anxiety, expectation, misery, anubhavas—lack of self-control, dullness of body, absent-mindedness, giving up washing the body, etc.

DAKSHINA NAYAKA (*Dakśina Nāyaka*): Nayaka whose affection is distributed. See *Nayaka*.

DANDAKARECHITA (*Daṇḍakarecita*) [NS]: See *Karana*.

DANDAPADA (*Daṇḍapāda*) [NS]: Akashiki chari; the foot held in Nupura chari is stretched, then turned quickly.

———— [NS]: Akashiki mandala; the right foot in Janita and Dandapada charis, the left in Suchi and Bhramari charis; again the right foot in Urudvritta chari, left foot in Alata chari, the right foot in Parshvakranta chari, left foot in Bhujangatrasita and Atikranta charis to meet the right foot in Dandapada chari and finally the left foot in Suchi and Bhramari charis.

——— [NS]: See *Karana*.

DANDAPAKSHA (*Daṇḍapakṣha*) [NS]: See *Karana*.

——— [NS]: Nritta hasta; two Hamsapaksha hands are moved near in and out either shoulder.

DARU (*Daru*): Musical composition consisting of sahitya, mridanga syllables, and swaras of the raga in which the daru is composed. The various types of darus are: kolatta, for singing and performing kolattam, patrapravesha, which serves to introduce a patra (character) in a dance drama especially Bhagavata mela and Kuchipudi; samvada, sung in the form of a dialogue; swagata daru, sung as a soliloquy; uttara-pratyuttara, sung in the form of a question-answer sequence; varnana, sung in praise of the hero (or any other important character).

DASARA PADA (*Dāsara Pada*): Padas or devotional songs steeped in bhakti bhava composed by devotees like Purandaradasa, Kanakadasa, Vijayadasa, Gopaladasa, Jagannathadasa.

DASHARUPAKA (*Daśarūpaka*): Treatise by Dhananjaya, written approximately towards end of tenth or beginning of eleventh century; deals in detail with natya, nritya, nritta, the five sandhis, nayaka-nayika classification, the various vrittis, and the ten rupakas.

———: The ten rupakas (dealt with in the treatise of the same name). These are: nātika, prakarana, bana, prahasana, dima, vyayoga, samavakāra, veethi, utshrishtikanka, ihāmriga and rasa.

DASHAVATARA HASTA (*Daśāvatāra Hasta*) [AD]: Hastas showing the ten incarnations of Vishnu—*Matsya:* Matsya hasta held at shoulder level. *Kurma:* Both hands Kurma held at shoulder level. *Varaha:* Varaha hasta held to the side at waist level. *Narasimha:* Left hand Simhamukha, right Tripataka at sides. *Vamana:* Left hand Mushti, near chest (suggesting holding an umbrella), right, also Mushti near waist (i.e. holding a kamandala). *Parashurama:* Left hand on waist, right, Ardhapataka at right side. *Rama:* Left hand Shikhara at left shoulder, right, Kapittha near right hip suggesting holding a bow. *Balarama:* Right hand Pataka, left Mushti at chest level. *Krishna:* Mrigashirsha hands facing each other, right thumb touching left little finger, held near the face, suggesting holding a flute. *Kalki:* Right hand Pataka, left, Tripataka held at either side chest level.

DASHTA (*Daṣṭa*) [NS]: Chibuka krama; lower lip is bitten by the teeth; denotes anger.

DEVATA HASTA (*Devatā Hasta*) [AD]: Hastas depicting gods and goddesses.

Brahma: Left hand Chatura or Alapadma, right, Hamsasya held at the sides. *Vishnu:* Both hands Tripataka at chest level, palms facing up and outward. *Shiva:* Left hand Alapadma at far left, right hand, Simhamukha held far out at right. *Lakshmi:* Both hands Kapittha at chest level. *Saraswati:* Right hand Suchi, held low down on right side, left, Kapittha at left shoulder. *Parvati:* Right hand Ardhachandra at right pointing down. Varada pose; left hand Ardhachandra at left side pointing up (Abhaya); both hands held with palms facing out. *Ganesha:* Both hands Kapittha held at waist level well away from the body suggesting a large waist. *Kartikeya:* Right hand Shikhara, left Trishula held at either side. Some writers interchange the hastas. *Manmatha:* Right hand Katakamukha and left hand Shikhara held in front at chest level. *Indra:* Right hand Kapittha, held up at right side, left hand held at left side in Tripataka. *Agni:* Right hand Tripataka and left, Kangula held in front at chest level. *Yama:* Right hand Suchi, left hand Pasha, held at chest level. *Nritti:* Right hand Shakata left hand Khatva. *Varuna:* Right hand Shikhara, left hand Pataka. *Vayu:* Right hand Arala, left Ardhapataka. *Kubera:* Right hand Kapittha [suggesting a mace (gada)], left hand Padmakosha.

DHANANJAYA (*Dhanañjaya*): Author of tenth or eleventh century treatise *Dasharupaka*.

DEEKSWASTIKA (*Dīkswastika*): See *Karana*.

DEENA (*Dīna*) [NS]: Drishti bheda expressing sthayi bhava of shoka; the eyelid is lowered slightly, eyeballs are slightly swollen and are moved slowly. Depicts sorrow.

DHEERA NAYIKA (*Dhīra Nāyikā*): Woman who speaks sarcastically to her erring lover. See *Nayika.*

DHEERADHEERA NAYIKA (*Dhīradhīra Nāyikā*): Woman who scolds her erring lover and cries simultaneously. See *Nayika.*

DHEERODATTA (*Dhīrodatta*): Nayaka who is strong, intelligent and compassionate. See *Nayaka.*

DHEERODHATTA (*Dhīrodhatta*): Nayaka who is proud, intolerant, hot-tempered, domineering; a wastrel. See *Nayaka.*

DHEERALALITA (*Dhīralalita*): Nayaka who is carefree, free from anxiety; is soft, pleasant, fond of easy living and pleasure. See *Nayaka.*

DHEERASHANTA (*Dhīrashānta*): Nayaka who is serene, cheerful, and self-reliant. See *Nayaka.*

DHRIṬI (*Dhṛṭi*) [NS]: Vyabhichari bhava of contentment. Vibhavas—heroism, spiritual knowledge, learning, wealth, purity, good conduct, devotion to one's superiors—acquiring money, enjoying sports; anubhavas—enjoying these things, not grumbling about things unattained, absence of fear, and sorrow.

DHRUVA TALA (*Dhruva Tāla*): Tala having sequence of one laghu, one druta and two laghus. See *Tala.*

DHUTA (*Dhūta*) [AD, NS]: Shirobheda; the head is shaken sideways, or moved from side to side. Denotes (AD) astonishment, sorrow, unwillingness, effects of cold and fever, first stages of intoxication, effort in battle, looking repeatedly to either side, saying 'it does not exist'; and (NS) unwillingness, sadness, astonishment, confidence, looking sideways, emptiness, and forbidding.

DOLA (*Ḍolā*) [AD]: Samyuta hasta; Pataka hands are moved to and fro loosely near the thighs.

———— : Hasta held by Nataraja's second left hand in the Nadanta pose. See *Nadanta.*

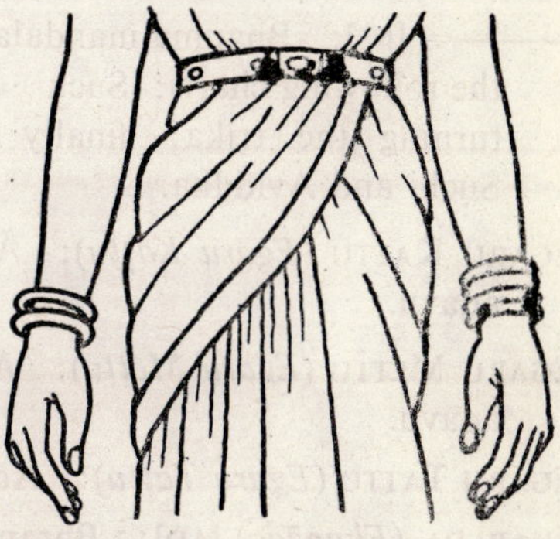

Dola

DOLAPADA (*Ḍolapāda*) [NS]: Akashiki chari; one Kunchita foot lifted, moved from side to side, then placed on the ground as Anchita.

——— [NS]: See *Karana.*

DRIPTA (*Dṛipta*) [NS]: Drishti bheda expressing sthayi bhava of utsaha; the eyes are opened wide and held motionless; depicts haughtiness.

DRISHTA NAYAKA (*Dṛṣṭa Nāyaka*): Nayaka who is guilty but craves forgiveness. See *Nayaka.*

DRISHTI BHEDA (*Dṛṣti Bheda*) [AD, NS]: Glances. AD: mentions 8—Alokita, Anuvritta, Avalokita, Nimilita, Pralokita, Sachi, Sama, Ullokita. NS: mentions in all 36. Of these 8 express rasas—Adbhuta, Bhayanaka, Bibhatsa, Hasya, Kanta, Karuna, Raudri, Veera; 8 express sthayi bhavas—Bhayanvita, Deena, Dripta, Hrishta, Jugupsita, Kruddha, Snigdha, Vismita; 20 express vyabhichari bhavas—Abhitapta, Akekara, Ardhamukula, Glana, Jihma, Kunchita, Lajjanvita, Lalita, Madira, Malina, Mukula, Shankita, Shranta, Sunya, Trasta, Vibhranta, Vikosha, Vipluta, Vishanna, Vitarkita.

DRUTA (*Druta*): One of the angas of tala, two akshara kalas; represented by a clap and a wave.

E

EDAKAKRIDITA (*Eḍakakrīḍita* [NS]: Bhaumi chari; jumping up and down with feet in Talasanchara.

——— [NS]: Bhauma mandala; both feet moved successively in the following charis: Suchi, Edakakridita, Bhramari, swiftly turning the trika; finally feet moved round alternately in Suchi and Aviddha.

EGARU KATTU (*Egaru Kaṭṭu*): Adavu; jumping and doing Kattu adavu.

EGARU METTU (*Egaru Meṭṭu*): Adavu; jumping and doing Mettu adavu.

EGARU TATTU (*Egaru Taṭṭu*): Adavu; jumping and stamping.

EKAPADA (*Ekapāda*) [AD]: Bhramari; moving round first on one foot, then on the other.

Alokita

Avalokita

Nimilita

Anuvritta (up)

Anuvritta (down)

Pralokita (Right)

Pralokita (Left)

Sachi

Sama

Ullokita

——— [AD]: Sthanaka; standing on one leg with the foot of the other leg on the knees of the first; denotes motionlessness, penance.

EKAPADATANDAVA (*Ekapādatānḍava*): Adavu; doing tandava with one foot, holding the other stationary.

EKA TALA (*Eka Tāla*): Tala having only one laghu. See *Tala.*

ELAKAKRIDITA (*Elakakrīḍita*) [NS]: See *Karana.*

G

GAJADANTA (*Gajadanta*) [NS]: Samyuta hasta; Sarpashirsha hands kept crossed and touching the fore-arms. Denotes

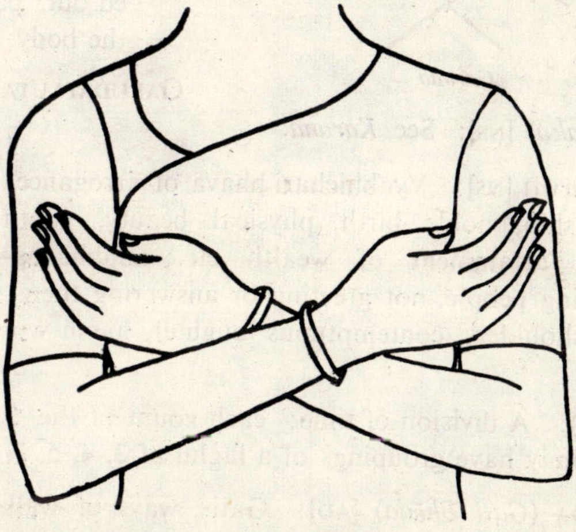

Gajadanta

carrying the bridegroom and the bride, great weight, clasping a pillar, uprooting a hill or boulder.

GAJAKRIDITA (*Gajakrīdita*) [NS]: See *Karana.*

GAJALILA GATI (*Gajalīlā Gati*) [AD]: Gati bheda of the elephant; walking slowly in Samapada, Pataka hands held at either side.

GANDA KRAMA (*Ganḍa Krama*) [NS]: Movements of the cheeks; 6 of these, viz., Kampita, Kshāma, Kunchita, Phulla, Purna, Sama.

GANDA SUCHI (*Ganḍa Sūci*) [NS]: See *Karana.*

GANGAVATARANA (*Gaṅgāvataraṇa*) [NS]: See *Karana*.

GARUDA (*Garuḍa*) [AD]: Bhramari; knee on the ground, moved round rapidly, with one foot stretched across the other and knee placed on the ground and body moved round rapidly.

——— [AD]: Sthanaka; one knee of Avidha posture is placed on the ground, both hands Tripataka, kept at either side.

——— [AD]: Samyuta Hasta; Ardhachandra hands with thumbs interlocked and fingers joined together and stretched out, palms facing the body.

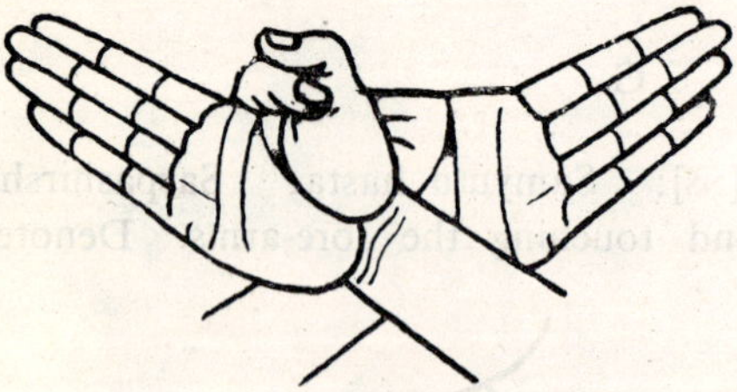

Garuda

GARUDAPLUTAKA (*Garuḍapluṭaka*) [NS]: See *Karana*.

GARVA (*Garva*) [NS]: Vyabhichari bhava of arrogance. Vibhavas —kingship, noble birth, physical beauty, youth, learning, power, attainment of wealth etc.; anubhavas—contempt, harassing people, not greeting or answering them, looking at one's shoulders, contemptuous laughter, harsh words, insults, etc.

GATI (*Gati*): A division of time: each count of the 5 jatis of a laghu may have groupings of a laghu of 3, 4, 5, 7, or 9 gatis.

GATI BHEDA (*Gati Bhēda*) [AD]: Gatis, ways of walking; 10 of these—Bhujanga, Gajalila, Hamsa, Manavi, Manduka, Mayura, Mriga, Simha, Turanga, Veera.

——— [NS]: Various gaits to express sentiments, for various types of people, animals and herds are described, but no specific technical terms given.

GATIMANDALA (*Gatimandala*) [NS]: See *Angahara*.

GHANA (*Ghana*): Musical instruments made of solid material, like cymbals etc. See *Sangeeta Vadya*.

GHATAM (*Ghaṭam*): Percussion instrument made of mud; a big mud-pot played with the fingers with the plam of the other hand held over its mouth.

GHURNITA (*Ghūrnita*) [NS]: See *Karana*.

GEETA (*Gīta*): Fundamental musical composition having both literary and musical content. Taught first in the study of music to enable the student to absorb the intricacies of a particular raga set to a particular tala.

GEETA GOVINDA (*Gīta Govinda*): Twelfth century Sanskrit poetical work in 24 ashtapadis by Jayadeva describing the love of Radha and Krishna, with the sakhi bringing the lovers together. Admirably suited to dance.

GLANA (*Glāna*) [NS]: Drishti bheda expressing vyabhichari bhava of laziness; eyebrows and eyelashes are moved slowly and the eyelids droop owing to fatigue.

GLANI (*Glāni*) [NS]: Vyabhichari bhava of weakness. Vibhavas—vomitting, purging, sickness, penance, austerities, fasting, mental worry, excessive drinking, sexual indulgence, travelling a long way, hunger, thirst, sleeplessness etc.; anubhavas—weak voice, lustreless eyes, pale face, slow gait, lack of energy, growing thin, change of colour etc.

GRIDHRAVALINAKA (*Gridhravalinaka*) [NS]: See *Karana*.

GREEVA BHEDA (*Grīva Bheda*) [AD, NS]: Neck movements. AD mentions 4—Parivartita, Prakampita, Sundari, Tiraschina. NS mentions 9—Anchita, Kunchita, Nata, Rechita, Sama, Tryasra, Unnata, Valita, Vivritta.

GREEVA RECHAKA (*Grīva Recaka*) [NS]: Rechaka; the neck is raised and lowered, then moved sideways describing a circle.

GURU (*Gurū*): Teacher.
One of the 6 angas of tala; it has 8 akshara kalas, i.e., 2 laghus.

H

HAMSA GATI (*Hamsa Gati*): Gati bheda of the swan; one foot placed slowly after the other at a distance of half a cubit; bending the body to either side, and hands in Tripataka on either side.

HAMSAPAKSHA (*Hamsapakṣa*) [AD, NS]: Asamyuta hasta; little finger of Sarpashirsha is stretched up, the other fingers joined

Hamsapaksha

and stretched out, thumb bent and kept at the side. Denotes (AD) number 6, constructing a bridge, marking with the nails, a covering or sheath, and (NS) pouring libations, accepting a gift, achamana, brahmans partaking of food, an embrace, a state of stupor, horripilation, touch, gentle massage, the prevailing sentiment, amorous action of women, relating to the region between the breasts, a sorrowful woman, touching a woman's chin.

HAMSASYA (*Hamsāsya*) [AD]: Asamyuta hasta; the thumb and index finger touch in a curve, the other fingers separated and stretched out straight; Denotes (AD) a blessing, a festival, tying something with thread, ascertaining, horripilation, pearls, pulling up a lamp wick, a touchstone, a jasmine, a pairting, the act of painting, dyke impeding a current.

Hamsasya

——— [NS]: Asamyuta hasta: forefinger, middle finger, and thumb are joined and the remaining fingers straightened and stretched out. Denotes saying 'especially' fine, small, loose, lightness, exist, softness.

HARINAPLUTA (*Hariṇapluṭa*) [NS]: Akashiki chari; after jumping, one foot is placed in Atikranta chari on the ground, the other foot in Anchita placed in Akshipta posture.

——— [NS]: See *Karana*.

HARSHA (*Harṣa*) [NS]: Vyabhichari bhava of joy. Vibhavas—attainment of a desired object, union with a loved one, mental satisfaction, receiving favours from the gods, or a preceptor, king, husband, master, receiving good food, clothing, money or enjoying these; anubhavas—brightness of face, and eyes, using sweet words, embracing, horripilation, tears, perspiration etc.

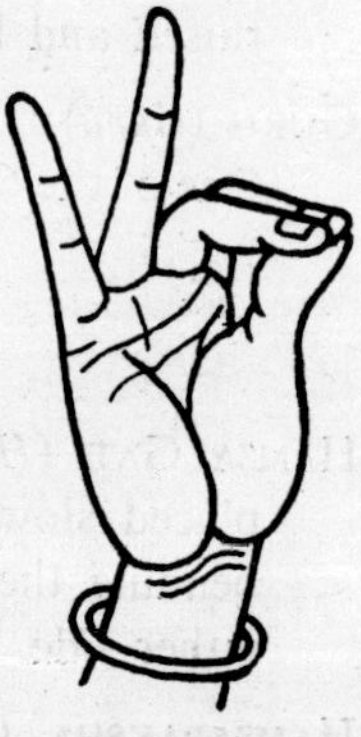

Hamsasya
(*also Katakamukha*)

HASITA (*Hāsita*) [NS]: An aspect of hasya rasa. Smiling with glowing eyes, face, cheeks; lips slightly parted and teeth visible, one of the six types of laughter.

HASTA (*Hasta*) [AD, NS]: Representative gestures with the hands classified as Asamyuta (using one hand) Samyuta (using both hands) and Nritta (used in nritta and adavu) hastas.

——— KARANA (———*Karaṇa*) [NS]: Hand movements; 4 in number—Aveshtita, Parivartita, Udveshtita, Vyavartita.

——— KSHETRA (——— *Kṣetra*): Position of hands in the performing of an adavu.

——— RECHAKA (——— *Recaka*) [NS]: Rechaka; the hand is raised up, thrown out and forward and turned round in a circular fashion.

HASYA (*Hāsya*) [NS]: Drishti bheda expressing hasya rasa. The eyelids are contracted alternately and the eyeballs moved so that they are slightly visible.

——— [NS]: Sthayi bhava of laughter; gives rise to hasya rasa; Vibhavas—mimicry, incoherent talk, foolishness; anubhavas—smiling, laughing.

——— RASA (——— *Rasa*) [NS]: Sentiment of comedy; presiding deity—Pramatha; sthayi bhava—laughter (hasya); representative colour—white; vibhavas—peculiar clothes, a defective limb, use of irrelevant words, mentioning different faults; anubhavas—throbbing of the lips, nose and cheeks, opening the eyes wide and contracting them, perspiration, reddening of the face, clutching the sides; vyabhichari bhavas—indolence, dissimulation, sleep, dreaming, insomnia, envy etc. Is of 2 kinds—centred in oneself, centred in others. Six varieties of laughter are listed—Smita, Hasita, Vihasita, Upahasita, Apahasita, Atihasita.

HAVA (*Hāva*): A slight external expression of bhava.

HRIDAYA KRAMA (*Hṛdaya Krama*) [NS]: Movements of the chest; 5 in number —Abhugna, Nirbhugna, Prakampita, Sama, Udvahita.

HRISHTA (*Hṛṣṭa*) [NS]: Drishti bheda expressing sthayi bhava of hasya; the eyes are slightly bent and moved, the eyeballs are not fully visible, eyelids are blinked; expresses joy.

J

Jadata (*Jaḍata*) [NS]: Vyabhichari bhava of stupor. Vibhavas—cessation of all activity, hearing of much desired thing or terrible thing, sickness etc.; anubhavas—speaking indistinctly, remaining silent, looking steadfastly, dependence on others etc.

Jangha Krama (*Jangha Krama*) [NS]: Movements of the shanks; 5 in number—Avartita, Kshipta, Nata, Parivritta, Udvahita.

Janita (*Janita*) [NS]: Bhaumi chari; one hand, Mushti is held at the chest, the other is moved round, feet kept in Talasanchara.

——— [NS]: See *Karana*.

Jaru (*Jaru*): Adavu; slipping one foot away from the other sideways or forwards; also Sarkal.

Jathara Krama (*Jaṭhara Kramą*) [NS]: Movements of the belly; 3 of these—Khalva, Kshama, Purna.

Jati (*Jāti*): Minute divisions of the time cycle; 5 of these, viz., tryasra or tisra, chaturashra (chatushra), khanda, mishra, sankeerna, containing 3, 4, 5, 7, and 9 akshara kalas, respectively. See *Tala*.

——— : Adavu; performing all adavus in the five fundamental jatis, i.e., tisra, chaturashra, khanda, mishra, sankeerna.

Jati (*Jati*): Combination of adavus in vilambita, madhya and druta (first, second and third) speeds, with different rhythm patterns involving 3, 4, 5, 7, and 9 beats and ending in odd numbers of Muktaya (Mudi) adavus.

Jatiswara (*Jatiswara*): Nritta item; swaras of any raga are set to various jatis in any tala and simple adavu patterns performed to this composition.

Javali (*Jāvali*): Musical composition in simple language, and generally set to madhya (middle) tempo containing pallavi, anupallavi and charanas, and suitable for abhinaya, especially delineation of shringara rasa.

Jayadeva (*Jayadēva*): Twelfth century Sanskrit poet; born in Kendubilva (modern Kenduli) in Bengal; devotee of Lord Krishna in whose honour he composed the poem *Geeta Govinda*. Also called Padmavati Charana Chārana Chakravarti (emperor of the movements of Padmavati's feet) by virtue of the fact that he made his wife, Padmavati, dance to his singing.

JYESHTA NAYIKA (*Jyeșța Nāyikā*): The elder wife. See *Nayika*.

JHAMPA TALA (*Jhampa Tāla*): Tala having a sequence of one laghu, one anudruta and one druta. See *Tala*.

JIHMA (*Jihma*) [NS]: Drishti bheda expressing vyabhichari bhava; lit. crooked; the eyelids are lowered slightly and contracted and the eyeballs concealed.

JUGUPSA (*Jugupsa*) [NS]: Sthayi bhava expressing disgust; gives rise to bibhatsa rasa. Vibhavas—seeing and hearing unpleasant things; anubhavas—contracting the body, spitting, narrowing the mouth.

JUGUPSITA (*Jugupsita*) [NS]: Drishti bheda expressing sthayi bhava of jugupsa (disgust); eyelids are contracted but not joined, eyeballs covered and drawn away from the object in view. Expresses disgust.

K

KAKAPADA (*Kākapada*): One of the 6 angas of tala; 4 laghus or 16 akshara kalas.

KALAHANTARITA (*Kalahāntarita*): Woman who first spurns her lover, then repents. One of the ashta nayikas. See *Nayika*.

KAMPA (*Kampa*): Satvika bhava; trembling caused by cold, fear, joy, anger, old age, the touch of a loved one. Also Vepathu.

KAMPANA (*Kampana*) [NS]: Adhara krama; trembling and throbbing of the lips to show pain, stiffness, cold, fear, anger etc.

——— [NS]: Uru krama; the heels are raised and lowered repeatedly; denotes the terrifying movement of persons of the inferior type.

KAMPITA (*Kampita*) [NS]: Ganda krama; trembling or throbbing of the cheeks; denotes anger, joy.

——— [AD, NS]: Shiro bheda; the head is nodded up and down; denotes (AD) taking offence, enquiry, hinting, calling someone, inviting deities, threatening someone, saying 'do stop' etc., and (NS) anger, argument, understanding, asserting, threatening, sickness, intolerance.

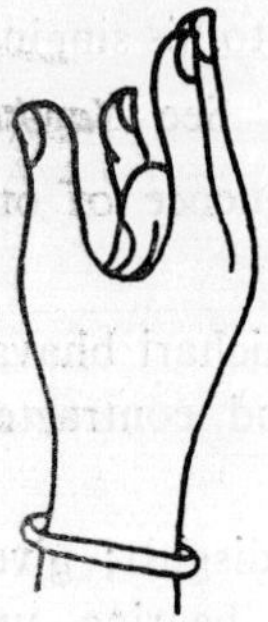
Kangula

KANGULA (*Kāngūla*) [AD, NS]: Asamyuta hasta; the third finger of Padmakosha is curved in. Denotes (AD) lakula fruit, a bell, bells worn by children, a partridge, a betelnut tree, small breast, white water lily, a chataka bird, a coconut and (NS) unripe fruit, woman's angry words. Also Langula.

KANISHTA (*Kaniṣṭa*): The younger (youngest) wife; the favourite. See *Nayika*.

KANJEERA (*Kañjīra*): Percussion instrument played with the fingers; it has a wooden frame with a skin stretched tight over it and circular metal discs around it.

KANTA (*Kānta*) [NS]: Drishti bheda expressing shringara rasa; a sidelong look with eyebrows and eyelashes contracted.

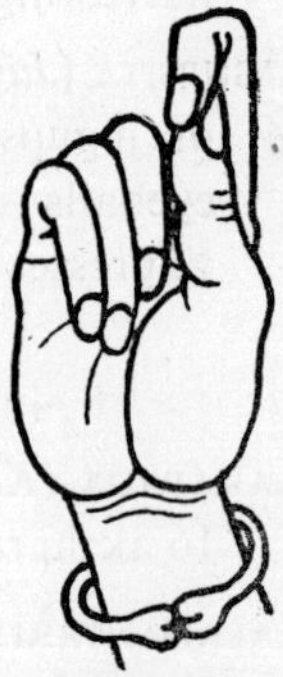
Kapittha

KAPITTHA (*Kapittha*) [AD, NS]: Asamyuta hasta; the forefinger of Shikhara is bent over the thumb and the bent little finger raised a little. Denotes (AD) Lakshmi, Saraswati, holding cymbals, milking cows, collyrium, holding flowers at the time of dalliance, grasping the ends of one's robes, offering incense or arati, and (NS) weapons (sword, bow, discus, javelin, spear, spike, thunderbolt, arrows), and good deeds.

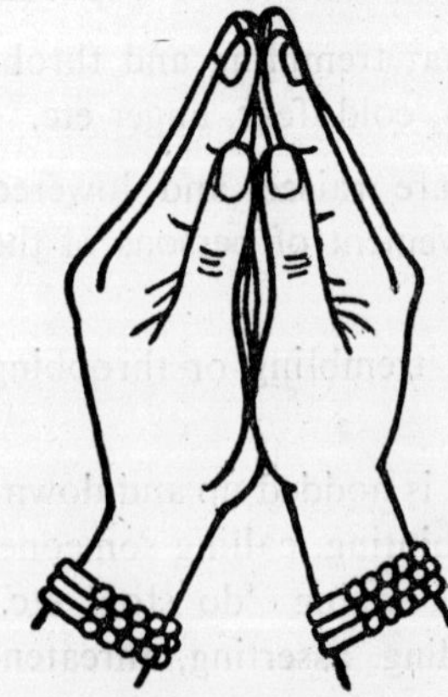
Kapota

KAPOTA (*Kapoṭa*) [AD, NS]: Samyuta hasta; Anjali hands joined with the palms hollowed out. Denotes (AD) salutation; addressing a preceptor, respectful acceptance or agreement, and (NS) approaching with an inimical attitude, bowing, talking to a venerable person, fear (in a woman).

KARANA (*Karanā*) [NS]: Dance movement using both feet and hands; combination of various sthanakas, charis and nritta hastas; forms the basis of adavus. Found depicted in stone carvings on the walls of passages in the gopurams of the Nataraja temple at Chidambaram. There are 108 in number. *Akshipta:* Lit. scattering; hands and feet moved about quickly. *Akshipta Rechita:* Lit. to cast off; left hand kept on chest, right hand Rechita, and then thrown up and sideways, then with both hands after performing Rechita with Apaviddha gestures performed. *Alata:* Lit. circling; the hand is brought down from shoulder and Urdhvajanu chari performed. *Anchita:* Lit. placing; in Ardhaswastika karana the Karihasta hand is moved in Vyavritta and Parivritta and then placed on the nose. *Apakranta:* Lit. oblique gait; thighs held in Valita, Apakranta chari performed with the feet, hands moved in harmony. *Apaviddha:* Lit. violently shaken; right hand Shukatunda kept on the upper side of the right thigh and the left hand on the chest. *Ardhamattali:* Lit. semi-intoxicated reeling; feet are drawn away from position in Skhalita karana, left hand Rechita, right hand on waist. *Ardhanikuttaka:* Lit. half-shouldered-arms; Alapallava hands placed bent on the shoulders and legs moved up and down. *Ardharechita:* Lit. the half whirl; Suchimukha hand moved freely, and the feet, alternately up and down, keeping the side in Sannata pose. *Ardhasuchi:* Lit. the half needle; right hand, Alapadma, placed over the head and the right foot in Suchipada karana. *Ardhaswastika:* Lit. legs crossed in Swastika; right hand Karihasta, and left hand kept on the chest. *Argala:* Lit. barred; one foot stretched back, two and half talas from the other, hands moved in conformity. *Atikranta:* Lit. the step forward; Atikranta chari performed and hands stretched forward, befittingly. *Avahittaka:* Lit. pointing fingers; Janita karana performed raising hands with fingers spread out, and then slowly let fall. *Avarta:* Lit. the whirlpool; Kunchita feet stretched out, body turned round in Avarta, hands moved in a befitting manner. *Bhramaraka:* Lit. the bee; with Swastika feet in Akshipta chari, the two hands are moved in Udveshtita turning the trika. *Bhujanganchita:* Lit. serpent touch; feet placed in Bhujangatrasita chari and Rechita performed with right hand and Lata with left hand. *Bhujangatrasita:* Lit. fear of a serpent; lift one bent leg, with the thigh in an oblique Nivartana movement and the waist and knees are arched out. *Bhujangatrasta-Rechita:* Reeling with bhujangatrasita; taking Bhujangatrasita chari with the feet and the two hands placed in Rechita to the left side. *Chakramandala:* Lit. turning the body; inner Apaviddha chari performed with body bent and held down between the two arms hanging straight. *Chatura:* Lit. four fingers; Anchita or Alapallava with left hand, Chatura with right hand and right foot kept in Kuttita pose. *Chinna:* Lit. split; Alapadma hands placed on the waist and then Vaishakha sthanaka taken. *Dandakarechita:* Lit. stiffened hands and legs; the hands and feet thrown freely about at sides and Rechita performed. *Dandapada:* Lit. stiff leg; Nupura chari performed, then a leg stretched out in Dandapada. *Dandapaksha:* Lit. stiff side; Urdhvajanu chari performed, and Lata hands kept in front of knees, then placed in Aviddhavakra. *Deekswastika:* Lit. crossed, sides; turning sideways and towards the front in one single movement, hands and feet are kept crossed in Swastika. *Dolapada:* Lit. swinging the leg; Kunchita foot lifted up and moved from side to side while swinging both hands. *Elakakridita:* Lit. Ram's sport; jumping up with Talasanchara feet, then dropping down, bending and twisting the body. *Gajakridita:* Lit. the sport of elephants; arched left hand brought near the left ear, right hand, Dola, near right ear and feet in Dolapada chari. *Gandasuchi:* Lit. Cheek-needle; feet kept in Suchi position, side in Unnata and one hand on the chest; and other hand bent to touch the cheek. *Gangavatarana:* Lit. descent of the Ganga; feet turned upwards, hands in Tripataka pointing downwards, and head in Sannata position. *Garudaplutaka:* Lit. the flight of Garuda; one leg stretched backward and hands at either side in Latarechita, chest raised. *Ghurnita:* Lit. reeling; right hand moving round in Valita, left hand in Dola, and drawing the feet away from Swastika position. *Gridhravalinaka:* Lit. Kite-like; one leg stretched backwards, the other knee bent slightly, hands stretched well out. *Harinapluta:* Lit. the flight of the deer; after performing Atikranta chari, jumping up and throwing down the leg and again bending one of the shanks and jumping. *Janita:* Lit. the origin; with one hand on the breast, and the other hanging loose, Janita chari is performed. *Karihasta:* Lit. the elephant's trunk; left hand placed on the chest, the right hand in Prodvestita and the legs in Anchita. *Katibhranta:* Lit. waist moved violently; the right leg in Suchi chari, right hand in Apaviddha and hip moved in Rechita. *Katichhinna:* Lit. split waist; the waist moved round with hands held over the head held in Pallava. Repeat the action frequently. *Katisama:* Lit. level waist; feet separated from Swastika position, one hand kept on the navel, the other on the hip and the sides in Udvahita pose. *Krantaka:* Lit. transit; bending Kunchita leg back, Atikranta chari is performed placing hands in Akshipta. *Kunchita:* Lit. angular bend; right leg bent back (nata) right hand kept bent as Kunchita and left hand at left side with palm up in Uttana. *Lalita:* Lit. graceful; left hand Karihasta, right hand turned to left side in Apavartita and the two feet moved up and down gracefully. *Lalatatilaka:* Lit. The forehead-mark; Vrischika karana with the right leg and with the big right toe the tilaka is marked on the forehead. *Latavrishchika:* Lit. Scorpion creeping down; right leg arched backwards in Anchita, left hand Lata on left side with palm and fingers bent and turned upwards. *Leena:* Lit. inserted; Anjali hands placed in front of chest, neck held high and shoulders back. *Lolitaka:* Lit. rolling; Rechita and Anchita performed with the two hands at the sides and head moved in Lolita and Vartita. Also Lolita. *Madaskhalita:* Lit. moving drunkenly; with hands hung down at sides, the head is tossed up in Parivahita and the feet turned round in Aviddha chari. *Mandalasvastika:* Lit. crossed region; hands kept in Swastika with palms and fingers turned up and towards the audience and body kept in Mandala sthanaka. *Matalli:* Lit. reeling drunkenly; throwing back the feet and making a whirling movement, hands are moved in Udveshtita and Apaviddha. *Mayuratilaka:* Lit. the peacock's grace; Vrischika karana with right leg, hands moved in Rechita and trika turned round. *Nagapasarpita:* Lit. serpentine movement; feet separated from Swastika position, head moved in Parivartita and the hands in Rechita. *Nikunchita:* Lit. bent; one leg lifted up in Vrischika karana and the two hands freely moved at the sides. *Nikuttaka:* Lit. shouldered arms; placing hands in Nikuttaka pose above the shoulders with some space between them and keeping the legs also in Nikuttaka pose. *Nisumbhita:* Lit. stamping; right leg bent back from behind, keeping the chest raised and the hand raised up on the forehead as Tilaka. *Nitamba:* Lit. posterior; Pataka hands lifted up with palms facing chest and Baddha chari performed with the feet. *Nivesa:* Lit. settling; hands kept on the chest which is in Nirbhugna, body in Mandala sthanaka. *Nupura:* Lit. the anklet; turning the trika round gracefully in Bhramara chari, keeping the hands in Lata and Rechita and moving the feet in Nupurapada chari. *Padapaviddhaka:* Lit. piercing the heels; keeping the two Katakamukha hands with their backs against the navel and doing Suchividdha and Apakranta charis. *Parivritta:* Lit. circling about; hands Apavestita; hands raised with feet in Suchi position, trika turned round. *Parshvajanu:* Lit. knee to one side; one foot kept in Sama position the opposite thigh raised and one hand held as Mushti on the chest. *Parvashvakranta:* Lit. movement to one side; Parshvakranta chari performed throwing hands out in front and moving them in a befitting manner. *Parshvanikuttaka:* Lit. folded arms on the sides; Swastika hands kept at the sides, feet in Nikutta. *Prasarpitaka:* Lit. moved to the front; one hand raised in Rechita, the other in Lata, and the feet kept in Talasanchara. *Prashtaswastika:* Lit. crossed at the back; the arms thrown up and bringing down in Swastika, keeping the two feet also crossed in Swastika doing Apakranta and Ardhasuchi charis. *Prenkholita:* Lit. cradle swing; performing Dola chari, then jumping up and bringing down the feet and moving the trika round. *Rechakanikuttaka:* Lit. whirling shouldered arms; right hand Rechita, left hand Dola and the right leg in Nikutta. *Samanakha:* Lit. level nails; legs placed stiff and straight and touching each other, both hands let down in Lata and body kept in natural straight pose. *Sambhranta:* Lit. bewilderment; one hand held in Avartita is placed arched over the right thigh which is in Aviddha. *Sannata:* Lit. hands well bent; jumping up and placing the legs in Swastika in front, at the same time keeping both hands in Dola at the sides. *Sarpita:* Lit. creeping serpent; arching the legs and moving forward keeping the head in Parivahita and the two hands in Rechita. *Shakatasya:* Lit. the cart wheel; curving the body back keeping the legs in Talasanchara till the feet are held with the hands. *Simhakarsita:* Lit. pulled by a lion; stretching one leg backwards, bending the hands and turning them round in front and bending again. *Simhavikridita:* Lit. lion's sport; Alata chari with the right leg, and then left leg moved quickly, moving the hands in harmony. *Skhalita:* Lit. tripped; Dolapada chari with the feet and hands turned round in Rechita. *Suchi:* Lit. needle; the Kunchita foot raised and put forward on the ground, and hands moved in harmony. *Suchividdha:* Lit. probing with a needle; right foot rested on the heel, left foot Suchipada piercing into the right, right hand kept on the waist and left, on the chest. *Swastika:* Lit. crossed; both hands and feet crossed. *Swastikarechita:* Lit. whirling cross; making Rechita and then Avidha with hands and then keeping them crossed as Swastika on the chest, then separating them and keeping them on the waist. *Talapushpaputa:* Lit. a handful of flowers; Pushpaputa hands on the left side, Agratalasanchara feet, Sannata pose. *Talasamghatita:* Lit. clapped palms; Dolapada chari performed with one leg, clapping and turning the left hand in Rechita. *Talasamsphotita:* Lit. clapping; lifting up one leg and stretching it forward, keeping the hands in Talasamsphotita gesture (as in clapping). *Talavilasita:* Lit. upturned toes; turning the toe and the sole of the foot upwards so that they are seen from the front and extending the leg on one side; hands are kept at sides with the palms bent downwards. *Udghatita:* Lit. standing on tip-toe; standing on the toes with hands in Talasamghatita and moving the waist to the sides. *Udvritta:* Lit. lifted up; keeping the body, hands and legs in Akshipta and doing Udvritta chari. *Unmatta:* Lit. frenzied; one leg bent in Anchita and the hands in Rechita. *Upasrita:* Lit. moved towards; Akshipta chari with one leg keeping the hands in harmony, body bent forward. *Urdhavajanu:* Lit. raised knee; Kunchita or bent leg lifted up and kept level with the chest; hands moved freely. *Uromandala:* Lit. chest region; the two feet are separated from the, Swastika position and Apaviddha chari performed keeping hands in Uromandala. *Urudvritta:* Lit. twisted thigh; making Avartita with one hand, then bending and placing it on the thigh, Anchita and Udvritta with the shanks. *Vaishakharechita:* Lit. whirling limb; body in Vaishakha sthanaka and hand and feet in Rechita. *Vaishakhaswastika*: Lit. crossed chest; legs in Swastika and Rechita hands on the chest bending the chest forward. *Valita:* Lit. folded in; hands in Apaviddha, feet in Suchi chari, trika turned round in Bhramari chari. *Valitoru:* Lit. folded thigh; with Shukatunda hands, Vyavartita and Parivartita is made with fingers over the chest, thighs in Valita. *Vartita:* Lit. inverted; with the hands slightly bent at the wrists, Avarta and Parivarta with the hands which are then lowered to the thighs with palms turned outwards, wrists slightly bent. *Vidyudbhranta:* Lit. a sudden flash; with leg held in behind in Valita, hands stretched out close to the head. *Vikshipta:* Lit. throwing about as above, but throwing hands and feet backwards and sideways. *Vikshiptakshipta:* Lit. thrown over; first throwing up the hands and feet (Vikshipta) and then throwing them down (Akshipta). *Vinivritta:* Lit. reversed Vivarta; Suchividdha chari with one leg, trika turned round with hands in Rechita. *Vishnukranta:* Lit. Vishnu's movement; one leg stretched in front and bent, as if on the point of walking; hands in Rechita. *Viskambha:* Lit. extended; Apaviddha performed with hand, Suchi chari with feet then leg kept in Nikutta and left hand kept on chest. *Vivartaka:* Lit. unfolding; throwing out the hands and feet in Akshipta, turning the trika round and making Anchita of the left hand. *Vivritta:* Lit. unwound; keeping the hands and feet in Akshipta, turning round the trika and then keeping the hands in Rechita. *Vrishabhakridita:* Lit. bull's sport; performing Alata chari with both hands Rechita, then Kunchita and Anchita. *Vrishchika:* Lit. scorpion; leg bent back and lifted up and then hands bent over the shoulders. *Vrishchikakuttita:* Lit. scorpion in Nikutta; assuming Vrischika karana with one leg with hands in Nikutta. *Vrishchikarechita:* Lit. whirling scorpion; Vrishchika karana with the leg, placing the two hands in Swastika, then making Rechita of the hands and separating them. *Vyamsita:* Lit. beguiled; taking Alidha sthanaka, and making both hands Rechita, placing them on the chest and moving them up and down.

KARIHASTA (*Karihasta*) [NS]: See *Karana*.

——— [NS]: Nritta hasta; one hand in Lata is held high up and moved from side to side, the other in Tripataka is held on the ear.

KARKATA (*Karkaṭa*) [AD, NS]: Samyuta hasta; fingers of the two hands interlocked, inwards or outwards. Denotes (AD) a multitude, the belly, filling a conch with wind, twisting and stretching limbs, pulling down a branch, and (NS) beeswax, massaging the limbs, yawning after awakening from sleep, a big body, supporting the chin, holding or blowing a conch.

Karkata

KARTARI (*Kartarī*) [AD]: Utplavana; leaping on toes with Kartari hands behind left foot, and simultaneously holding a downward Shikhara, on waist.

KARTARIMUKHA (*Kartarīmukha*) [AD, NS]: Asamyuta hasta; index and middle fingers of Ardhapataka or Tripataka separated and stretched. Denotes (AD) separation of man and woman, overturning, opposition, plundering, corner of the eye, death, estrangement, lightning, sleeping alone during separation, falling, weeping; and (NS) showing the way, decorating the feet, dyeing the feet, crawling of babies, biting, a horn, letters, falling down, death, transgression, reversion, cogitation, putting in trust.

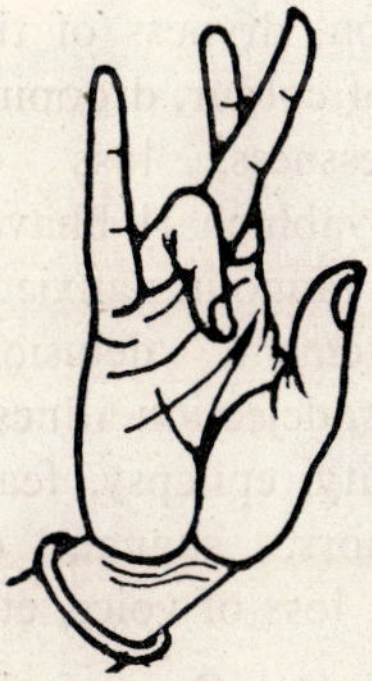

Kartarimukha

KARTARISWASTIKA (*Kartarīswastika*) [AD]: Samyuta hasta; two

Kartarimukha hands crossed in Swastika at the wrists; denotes branches, hill-tops, trees.

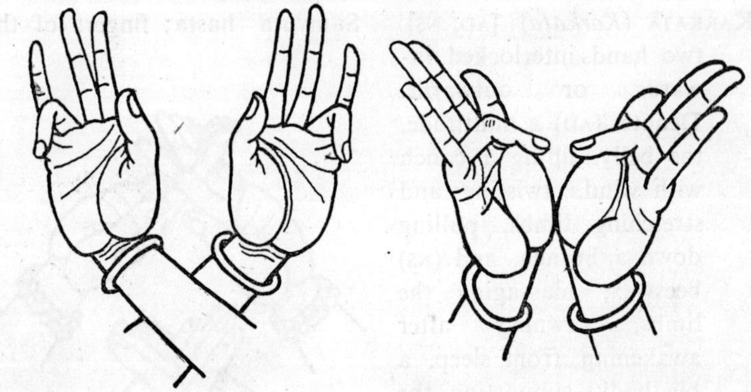

Kartariswastika

KARUNA (*Karuṇa*) [NS]: Drishti bheda expressing Karuna rasa; the upper eyelid is lowered, the eyeball is at rest owing to mental agony, gaze fixed at the tip of the nose.

——— RASA (——— *Rasa*) [NS]: Sentiment of pathos; presiding deity, Yama; sthayi bhava, shoka; representative colour, ash-grey. Vibhavas—affliction under a curse, separation from dear ones, loss of wealth, death, captivity, flight from one's house, accidents, misfortune; anubhavas — shedding tears, lamentation, dryness of the mouth, change of colour, drooping limbs, breathlessness, loss of memory etc.; vyabhichari bhavas —indifference, langour, anxiety, yearning, excitement, delusion, fainting, sadness, dejection, illness, inactivity, insanity, epilepsy, fear, paralysis, tremors, change of colour, weeping, loss of voice, etc.

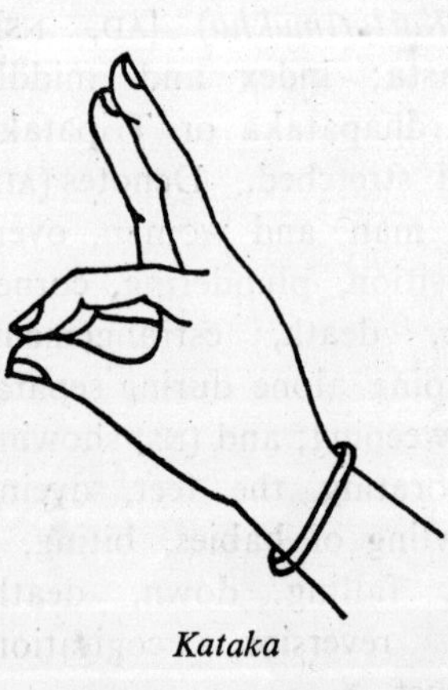

Kataka

KATAKA (*Kataka*) [AD]: One of the 4 extra asamyuta hastas; the middle and ring fingers of the Samdamsha hand are raised, the rest joined. Denotes calling, moving. Rarely used nowadays.

KATAKAMUKHA (*Katakāmukha*) [AD]: Asamyuta hasta; the index and middle fingers of Kapittha are joined to the thumb and the other two fingers may be separated and stretched out. Denotes picking flowers, holding a pearl necklace or garland of flowers, drawing a bow-string, offering betel leaves, preparing paste of musk or sandal by rubbing them against something, applying perfume, speaking, glancing. The hasta corresponds to Hamsasya of NS. (See *Hamsasya.*)

——— [NS]: Asamyuta hasta; the third and little finger of Kapittha are raised and bent. Denotes sacrifice, oblation, umbrella, drawing up reins, fan, holding a mirror, drawing patterns, powdering, taking up big sticks, arranging a pearl necklace, picking up a garland, gathering the ends of one's clothes, churning, shooting arrows, plucking flowers, wielding a goad or drawing out a goad, a string, looking at a woman.

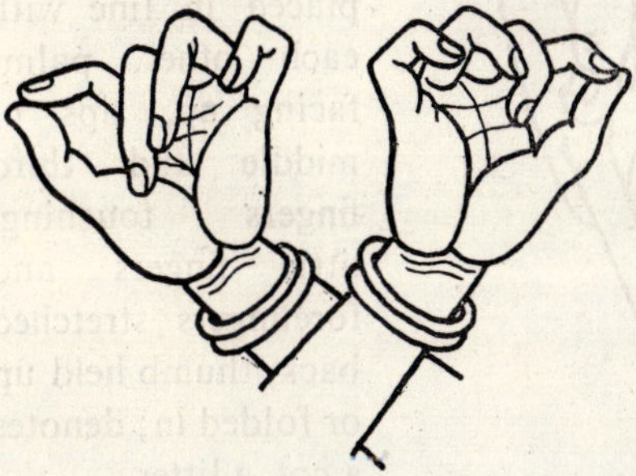

Katakavardhamanaka

KATAKAVARDHAMANA (*Kaṭakavardhamāna*) [AD]: Samyuta hasta; two Katakamukha hands are crossed at the wrists in Swastika. Denotes, coronation, worshipping, marriage.

KATAKAVARDHAMANAKA(*Kaṭakavardhamānaka*)[NS]: Samyuta hasta as above denotes movements in love-making; also used when bowing.

KATIBHRANTA (*Kaṭibhrānta*) [NS]: See *Karana*.

KATICHHINNA (*Kaṭichhinna*) [NS]: See *Karana*.

KATI KRAMA (*Kaṭi Krama*) [NS]: Movements of the waist; 5 in number — Chinna, Nivritta, Prakampita, Rechita, Udvahita.

KATI RECHAKA (*Kaṭi Recaka*) [NS]: Rechaka; the trika is raised up and the waist turned round by drawing it back.

KATISAMA (*Kaṭisama*) [NS]: See *Karana*.

KATTU (*Kaṭṭu*): Adavu; cross one foot resting on the toes, behind the other.

KESHABANDHA (*Keśabandha*) [NS]: Nritta hasta; the hands are moved outwards from the hair-knot and held on the sides.

KHALVA (*Khalva*) [NS]: Jathara krama; the belly is depressed. Denotes sickness, penance, weariness and hunger.

KHANDA (*Khaṇḍa*): Movement comprising 3 karanas.

———JATI (———*Jāti*): A laghu of 5 akshara kalas.

KHANDANA (*Khaṇḍana*) [NS]: Chibuka krama; the two lips come together repeatedly. Denotes muttering prayers, studying, speaking, eating.

KHANDITA NAYIKA (*Khaṇḍita Nāyikā*): A jealous angry woman. See *Nayika*.

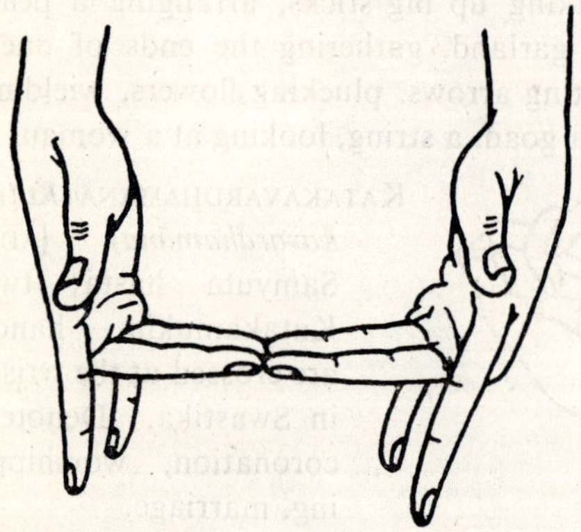

Khatva

KHATVA (*Khaṭva*) [AD]: Samyuta hasta; two Chatura hands are placed in line with each other, palms facing up, tips of middle and third fingers touching, little fingers and forefingers stretched back, thumb held up or folded in; denotes a cot, a litter.

KILAKA (*Kilaka*) [AD]: Samyuta hasta; the little fingers of two Mrigashirsha hands are interlocked, denotes friendship, affection, joyous talk.

KINKINI (*Kinkiṇi*): String of bells tied on the feet by dancers.

KRANTA (*Krānta*) [NS]: Akashiki mandala; the following charis are performed in all directions, right foot in Suchi, left in Apakranta, then both feet in Parshvakranta, moving round in all directions, then left foot in Suchi, right foot

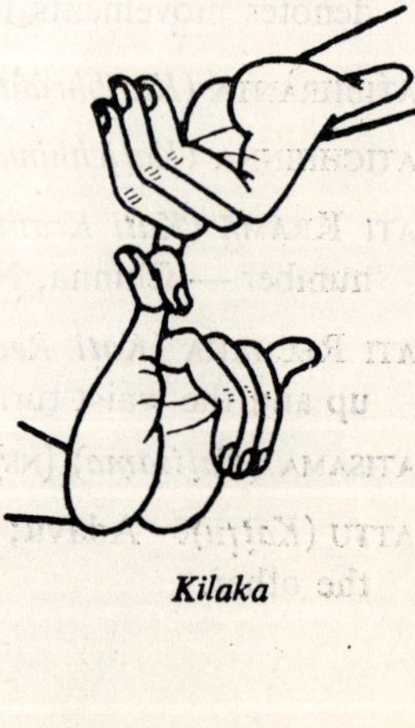

Kilaka

in Apakranta. This mandala is used for the natural gait hence it is called Kranta or 'going'.

KRANTAKA (*Krāntaka*) [NS]: See *Karana*.

KRIPALAGA (*Kripālaga*) [AD]: Utplavana; leaping with each heel alternately touching the hip, and keeping Ardhachandra hands between the feet.

KRODHA (*Krodha*) [NS]: Sthayi bhava of anger; gives rise to raudra rasa; vibhavas—insolence, abusive language, quarrels; anubhavas—swollen nose, upturned eyes, biting the lips, throbbing of the cheeks etc.

KRUDDHA (*Kruddha*) [NS]: Drishti bheda expressing sthayi bhava of krodha (anger); the eyes are motionless and drawn up, eyeballs are immobile and turned up, eyebrows are knitted.

KSHAMA (*Kṣāma*) [NS]: Ganda krama; cheeks are depressed; denotes sorrow.

——— [NS]: Jathara krama; the belly is made thin; denotes laughter, weeping, inhalation, yawning.

KSHIPTA (*Kṣipta*) [NS]: Jangha krama; the shanks are thrown out; used in the exercise of limbs.

KSHETRANGNA (*Kṣetrangña*): Seventeenth century Telugu composer, born Muvvapuri in Andhra, and author of many shringara padas, all containing the ankita nama 'Muvva Gopala'. He is called this because of the legend that he visited many kshetras. Also called Padachakravarti because of his mastery of bhava, raga and laya.

KUNCHITA (*Kuñcita*) [AD]: Bhramari; moving round with bent knees.

——— [NS]: Bhru chalana; contracted brows—the eyebrows are slightly bent one by one or both at the same time; denotes manifestation of love, pretence, hysteria.

——— [NS]: Drishti bheda expressing vyabhichari bhava; the eyelashes are bent owing to the eyelids being contracted, and the eyeballs are also contracted.

——— [NS]: Ganda krama; cheeks are contracted or narrowed; denotes horripilation, sensitive touch, cold, fear, fever.

——— [NS]: Greeva bheda, the neck and head are bent down; denotes pressure owing to weight, protecting the neck.

——— [NS]: See *Karana*.

——— [NS]: Pada krama; the heels are thrown up, toes bent down, middle part of the foot is also bent; denotes the aristocratic way of walking, turning to the right or left; it is also used in Atikranta chari.

——— [NS]: Puta chalana; contracted eyelids; denotes seeing some undesirable object, fragrance, flavour, touch.

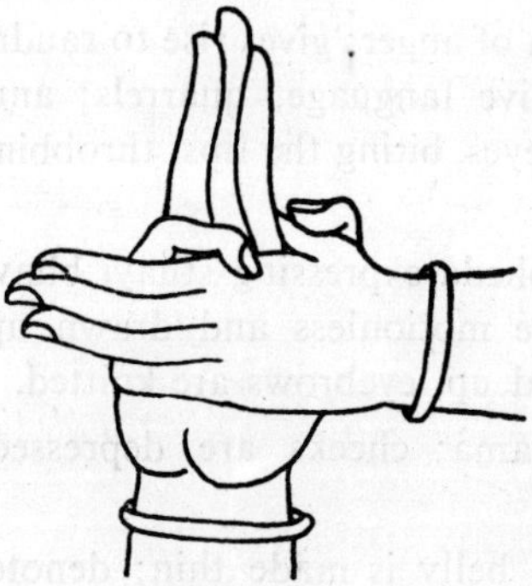

Kurma

KURMA (*Kūrma*) [AD]: Samyuta hasta; the tips of the thumbs and little fingers of Chakra are bent; denotes a tortoise. See also *Dashavatara Hasta*.

KUṬṬANA (*Kuṭṭana*) [AD]: Chari; the ground is struck with one heel or forefoot or the entire sole of one foot.

——— [NS]: Chibuka krama; upper teeth brought in conflict with lower ones; denotes fear, cold, attack of sickness, old age.

L

LAGHU (*Laghū*): One of the angas of tala, represented by a clap followed by counting on fingers; the number of fingers counted depends on the laghu. Thus: tisra—a clap and 2 counts (total 3), chaturashra—a clap and 3 counts (total 4), khanda—a clap and 4 counts (total 5), mishra—a clap and 6 counts (total 7), sankeerna—a clap and 8 counts (total 9). See also *Tala*.

LAJJANVITA (*Lajjanvita*) [NS]: Bashful; drishti bheda expressing vyabhichari bhava. The eyelashes are slightly lowered, and the upper eyelids and eyeballs lowered in shyness.

LALATATILAKA (*Lalatatilaka*) [NS]: See *Karana*.

LALITA (*Lalitā*) [NS]: Akashiki mandala; the following charis are performed in succession; Suchi with the right foot, left moved in Apakranta, right in Parshvakranta and Bhujangatrasita, left in Atikranta, Urudvritta and Alata, right in Parshvakranta and left with graceful steps in Atikranta.

——— [NS]: Amorous; drishti bheda expressing vyabhichari bhava. The eyes are contracted at the ends as in smiling and the eyeballs are moved.

——— [NS]: See *Karana*.

——— [NS]: Nritta hasta; two Alapallava hands are crossed above the head.

LALITASANCHARA (*Lalitasañcāra*) [NS]: Akashiki mandala; the following charis are performed in succession: Suchi with the right knee raised, left in Apakranta, right in Parshvakranta, left in Suchi and Bhramari, right again in Parshvakranta, left Atikranta and Bhramari.

LANGULA (*Lāngula*) [AD]: Asamyuta hasta. See *Kangula*.

LASYA (*Lāsya*): Graceful dance; generally having shringara as the dominant rasa. The opposite of Tandava which is majestic and powerful.

LASYA RANJANA (*Lāsya Rañjana*): Sixteenth century treatise on dance by King Simhabhupala. (Trans. Kannada and English, Oriental Research Institute, Mysore University).

LATA (*Latā*) [NS]: Nritta hasta; both hands moved obliquely at the sides.

LATAVRISCHIKA (*Latāvṛścika*) [NS]: See *Karana*.

LAYA (*Laya*): Tempo in music or dance; tempo in which a tala is played. May be vilambita, madhya or druta.

——— : Panchakriya of Nataraja; destruction as represented by fire held in one left hand of the Nadanta pose. Also Samhara. See *Nadanta*.

LEHITA (*Lehita*): Chibuka krama; chin is held in such a position that the lips and tongue touch. Depicts greed.

LEENA (*Līna*) [NS]: See *Karana*.

LOKADHARMI (*Lokadharmi*): Realistic dance or gestures that express one's feelings or tell about some external object. The opposite of Natyadharmi which is conventional and idealistic.

LOLITA (*Lolita*) [AD]: Chari; after performing Kuttanachari the foot is not allowed to rest on the ground, but is moved slowly.

——— [NS]: Shiro bheda; the head is turned round and round. Denotes fainting, intoxication, sickness, drowsiness.

——— [NS]: See *Lolitaka.*

LOLITAKA (*Lolitaka*) [NS]: See *Karana.*

LUTHIKA (*Luthika*) [AD]: Chari; Kuttana chari performed with feet in Swastika position.

M

MADA (*Mada*) [NS]: Vyabhichari bhava of drunkenness. Vibhavas—imbibing liquor etc. (NS. mentions five vibhavas but does not enumerate them); anubhavas—intoxication of three kinds: *light* (characterised by smiles, mild euphoria, slightly faltering speech and gait and relating to persons of the superior type, who, in such a condition, sleep), *medium* (characterised by rolling eyes, drooping arms, unsteady gait and relating to persons of the middle type, who, in such a condition, laugh and sing), and *excessive* (characterised by loss of memory, a thick protruding tongue, inability to walk, vomiting, hiccoughing, coughing, spitting and relating to persons of the inferior type, who, in such a condition, cry and use angry words).

MADASKHALITA (*Madaskhalita*) [NS]: See *Karana.*

MADIRA (*Madira*) [NS]: Intoxicated; drishti bheda expressing vyabhichari bhava of mada (drunkenness). The eyeballs are rolled, the ends of the eyes contracted, the eyes are then bent and the corners fully opened.

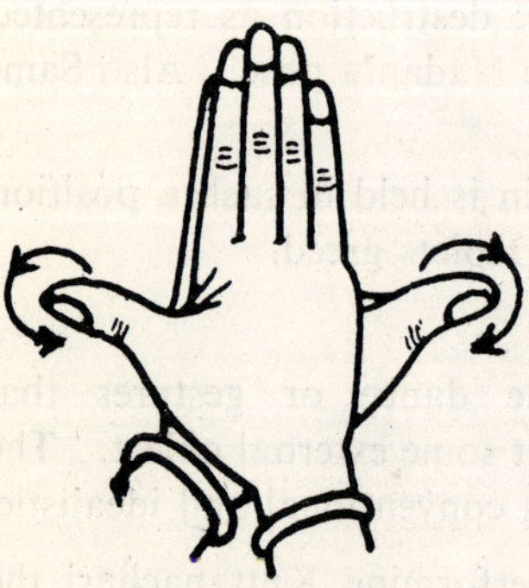

Makara

MADAVILASITA (*Madavilāsita*) [NS]: See *Angahara.*

MADHYAMA NAYIKA (*Madhyama Nāyikā*): A nayika who returns good for good and evil for evil. See *Nayika.*

MAI (*Mai*): Adavu; bending the body.

MAKARA (*Makara*) [NS]: Samyuta hasta; two Pataka hands with thumbs separated and held palm downwards one on top of the other. Denotes lion, tiger, elephant, crocodile, shark, and any other carnivorous animals. See also *Matsya.*

MALINA (*Malina*) [NS]: Pale; drishti bheda expressing vyabhichari bhava. The ends of the eyelids are held motionless, the ends of the eyes are pale, lids are half-closed.

MANAVI GATI (*Mānavi Gati*) [AD]: Gati bheda of Hanuman; going round in quick steps with left hand at waist and right Katakamukha at chest.

MANDA (*Manda*) [NS]: Nasika krama; nostrils held at rest. Depicts discouragement, anxiety, impatience.

MANDALA (*Maṇḍala*) [AD]: Standing postures; 10 of these—Alidha, Ayata, Mottita, Parshvasuchi, Pratyalidha, Prenkhana, Prerita, Samasuchi, Sthanaka, Swastika.

——— [NS]: Sequences formed by the combination of charis; a combination of 4 khandas. Two types; viz. akashika mandalas and bhauma mandalas.

——— [NS]: Sthanaka; the feet are kept 4 talas apart, obliquely, then turned sideways; waist and knees are held in the natural position; used in drawing of bow, thunderbolt, riding on an elephant, mimicking big birds.

MANDALASWASTIKA (*Maṇḍalaswastika*) [NS]: See *Karana*.

MANDI (*Maṇḍi*): Adavu; placing the knees on the ground.

MANDUKA GATI (*Maṇḍūka Gati*) [AD]: Gati bheda of the frog; standing on toes and jumping forward holding Shikhara hands together.

MARANA (*Maraṇa*) [NS]: Vyabhichari bhava depicting death. Vibhavas—sickness or injury; anubhavas—(in case of sickness) loss of physical control, clouded eyes, hiccoughing, breathing deeply, looking for other members of the family, speaking indistinctly, and (in the case of injury) falling to the ground, loss of weight, tremors, burning sensation, foaming at the mouth, breaking the neck, paralysis, and absence of any movement.

MATI (*Mati*) [NS]: Vyabhichari bhava of assurance; vibhavas—considering the meaning of the Shastras or the pros and cons of a matter; anubhavas—instructing students, ascertaining the meaning of something, removal of doubts, etc.

MATSYA (*Matsya*) [AD]: Samyuta hasta; two Pataka hands placed palm downwards on top of each other; with thumbs held out and rotated. Denotes a fish. See also *Makara; Dashavatara Hasta.*

MATTAKRIDA (*Maṭṭakrīḍā*) [NS]: See *Angahara.*

MATTALI (*Mattali*) [NS]: Bhaumi chari; moving backwards with a circular movement with hands held motionless in Udveshtita.

——— [NS]: See *Karana.*

MATTASKHALITA (*Maṭṭaskhalita*) [NS]: See *Angahara.*

MATTHYA TALA (*Maṭṭhya Tala*): Tala having a sequence of one laghu, one druta and one laghu. See *Tala.*

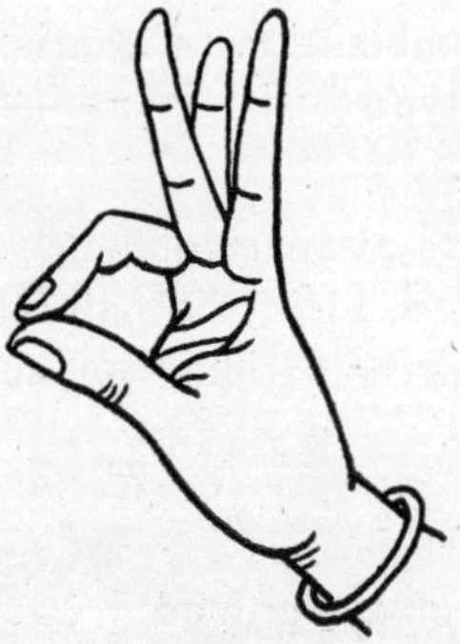

Mayura

MAYURA (*Mayūra*) [AD]: Asamyuta hasta; the ring-finger and thumb in Tripataka are joined and the other fingers are extended. Denotes a peacock, peacock's neck, creeper, bird, vomitting, removing hair, tilaka mark, river water being rippled, discussing the shastras, fame.

MAYURA GATI (*Mayūra Gati*) [AD]: Gati bheda of the peacock; moving forward on toes; knees held in front, hand held alternately in Kapittha.

MAYURATILAKA (*Mayūratilaka*) [NS]: See *Karana.*

METTU (*Meṭṭu*): Adavu; placing first the toes on the ground, then the heels.

MISHRA JATI (*Miśra Jāti*): Laghu possessing 7 akshara kalas.

MOHA (*Moha*) [NS]: Vyabhichari bhava of distraction. Vibhavas—accidental injury, adversity, sickness, fear, agitation, remembering, an enemy; anubhavas—lack of, or excessive movement; falling down, reeling, inability to see properly, etc.

MOTTITA (*Moṭṭita*) [AD]: Mandala; both hands Tripataka, toes touching the ground, and the knees are touched to the ground alternately.

MRIDANGA (*Mṛdaṅga*): Percussion instrument comprising a hollow wooden drum covered on both sides with skin and played with the fingers and palm.

MRIGA GATI (*Mṛga Gati*) [AD]: Gati bheda of the deer; running forward or sideways holding Tripataka hands.

MRIGASHIRSHA (*Mṛgaśīrṣa*) [AD, NS]: Asamyuta hasta; the thumb and forefinger of Sarpashirsha are lifted up, the other fingers are straightened and extended. Denotes woman, cheek, a wheel, limit, fear, quarrel, dress or costume, calling, tilaka, deer, lute, massaging the feet, getting everything, female organ, holding an umbrella, stepping.

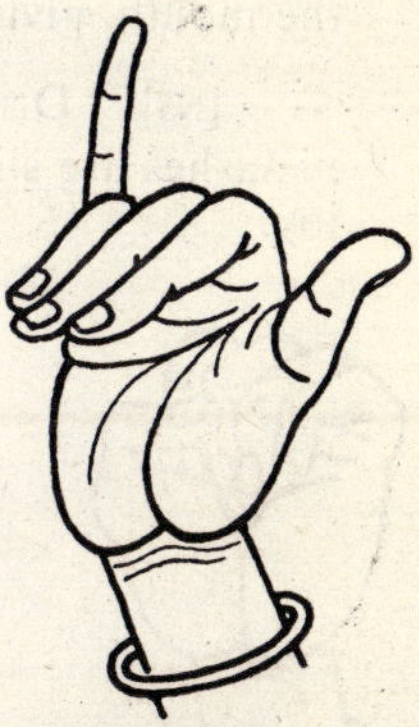
Mrigashirsha

MUDI (*Muḍi*): See *Muktaya.*

MUGDHA NAYIKA (*Mugdha Nāyikā*): Young girl at the inception of youth and love. See *Nayika.*

MUKHA BHEDA (*Mukha Bheda*) [NS]: Movements of the mouth. Six in number—Bhugna, Nirbhugna, Udvahi, Vidhuta, Vinivritta, Vivritta.

MUKHAJA (*Mukhaja*): Abhinaya using the face. See *Angikabhinaya.*

MUKHA RAGA (*Mukha Rāga*) [NS]: Colour of the face; 4 in number—Prasanna, Rakta, Swabhavika, Shyama.

MUKTAYA (*Muktaya*): A rhythmic pattern in units of 3 (such as Tadiginatom—Tadiginatom—Tadiginatom) played on percussion instruments towards the end of a jati or teermanam; also towards the end of an avartana of a tala. The beat immediately following the muktaya sequence corresponds to the first beat of the next avartana. Can also be played in units of 1, 5, 7 and 9.

———: Adavu; performed towards the end of a dance sequence usually 3, 5, 7 or 9 times. Also called Mudi.

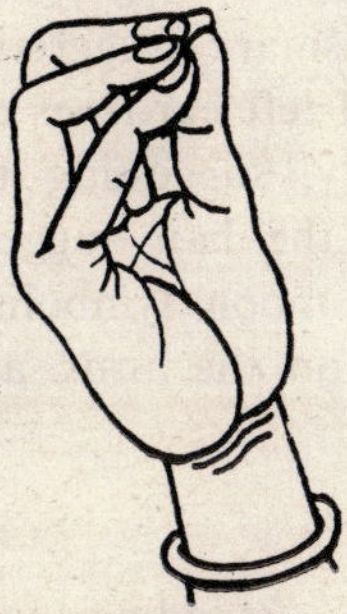
Mukula

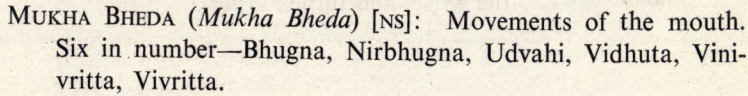

MUKULA (*Mukula*) [AD, NS]: Asamyuta hasta; the fingers are joined together. Denotes (AD) water lily, eating, god of love (with 5 arrows), holding a signet or seal, navel, plantain flower; and (NS) water lily, throwing a kiss, contempt, miscellaneous things, eating, counting gold coins, narrowing the mouth, giving away something, quickness, flower buds.

———— [NS]: Drishti bheda expressing vyabhichari bhava; the eyelashes are slightly fluttered and the eyelids opened. Shows joy.

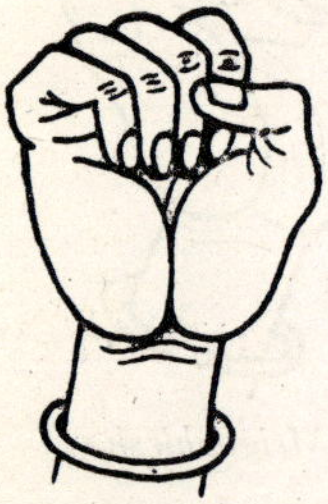

Mushti

MUSHTI (*Muṣṭī*) [AD, NS]: Asamyuta hasta; the fingers are closed into a fist and the thumb placed over them. Denotes (AD) steadfastness, grasping the hair, holding things, wrestlers fighting, and (NS) exercise, exit, pressing, washing, grasping a sword, holding a club or a spear.

MUSHTIKASWASTIKA (*Muṣṭikaswastika*) [NS]: Nritta hasta; two Katakamukha hands are bent at the wrists and turned around.

N

NADANTA (*Nadanta*): Shiva's cosmic dance depicting also Hindu philosophy. Represented in sculpture thus—of the two right hands, one holds a drum (or deer) suggesting creation (shrishti) and the other is in Abhaya hasta (sthiti or protection); of the two left hands, one holds fire (laya or samhara or destruction), and the other is in Dola hasta; the left foot's big toe is raised to show anugraha (salvation) and the base of the icon is a Shrichakra (6-pointed star suggesting tirobhava or illusion). These five concepts are the panchakriyas. The right foot tramples on the demon Muyalaga or Apasmara (suggesting the trampling down of evil). The right and left ear-rings are those of a man and a woman, respectively, suggesting the union of man and woman. The Ganga in the hair suggests the eternal flow of life, and the crescent moon symbolises dharma and wisdom, while the serpents on the arms and neck suggest the tying down of evil.

NADE (*Naḍé*): Adavu; ways of walking.

NAGABANDHA (*Nāgabandha*) [AD]: Sthanaka; standing with hands and legs intertwined. Denotes serpents.

——— [AD]: Samyuta hasta; Sarpashirsha hands are crossed at the wrists in Swastika.

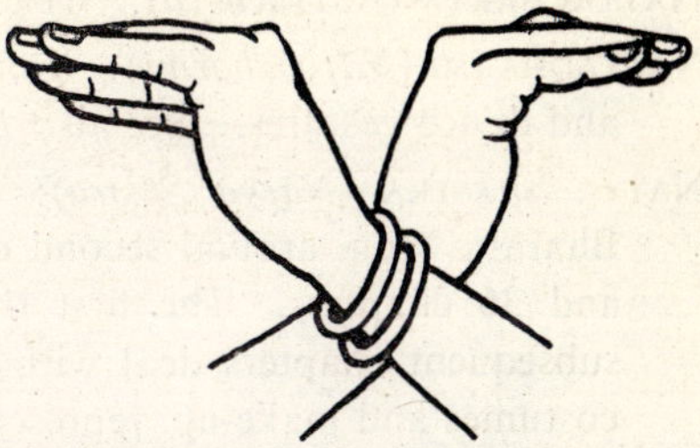

Nagabandha

NAGAPASARITA (*Nāgapasarita*) [NS]: See *Karana*.

NALINIPADMAKOSHA (*Nalinipadmakoṣa*) [NS]: Nritta hasta; hands are moved alternately in Vyavartita and Parivartita karanas.

NANDIKESHWARA (*Nandikeśwara*): Author of *Abhinaya Darpana* and *Bharatarnava*, treatises on Bharata Natya.

NARTAKA (*Nartaka*): Male dancer.

NARTAKI (*Nartakī*): Female dancer.

NARTANA (*Nartana*): Comprehensive term for nritta, nritya and natya.

NASIKA KRAMA (*Nāsika Krama*) [NS]: Movements of the nose; 6 of these—Manda, Nata, Suchhvasa, Swabhavika, Vikrishta, Vikunita.

NATA (*Nata*): Male dancer or actor.

——— [NS]: Greeva bheda; the neck and face are bent down. Denotes wearing ornaments, embracing.

——— [NS]: Jangha krama; the knees are bent. This posture is assumed in certain sthanakas and asanas.

——— [NS]: Nasika krama; nostrils are retracted. Denotes weeping when performed repeatedly.

——— [NS]: Parshva krama; the waist is slightly bent and one shoulder is drawn away. Assumed when approaching someone.

NATARAJA (*Naṭarāja*): Shiva as Lord of Dance, represented by Nadanta pose. See *Nadanta*.

NATI (*Nati*): Female dancer or actress.

NATU (*Nāṭu*): Adavu; stretching and placing heel on the ground; toes facing upwards.

NATYA (*Nāṭya*): Originally representation of rasa through chaturvidha abhinaya; now indicates a dance-drama through the medium of any of the classical dance styles.

NATYACHARYA (*Nāṭyācārya*): Teacher of dance.

NATYADHARMI (*Nāṭyadharmi*): Conventional and idealistic dance and dance gestures. See also *Lokadharmi*.

NATYA SHASTRA (*Nāṭya Śāstra*): Treatise on natya written by Bharata Muni around second century. Contains 6,000 verses and 36 chapters. The first thirteen chapters are on dance, subsequent chapters deal with rules of prosody, plays, styles, costumes and make-up, representation of dramatic production, music and musical instruments, talas, etc.

NATYA SHASTRA SANGRAHA (*Nāṭya Śāstra Saṅgraha*): Important sections of Natya Shastra compiled in Marathi by Utake Govindachary on the orders of the Maratha kings of Tanjore (Saraswati Mahal Library, Tanjore, edns. in Marathi and trans. in Tamil and English).

NAVAGRAHA HASTA (*Navagṛha Hasta*) [AD]: Hastas depicting the 9 heavenly bodies: *Surya*: Sun; left hand Alapadma and right hand, Kapittha held at chest. *Chandra:* Moon; left, Alapadma and right, Pataka held at chest. *Kuja:* Mars; left, Suchi and right, Mushti held horizontally. *Budha*: Mercury; left, Mushti and right, Pataka held horizontally. *Guru:* Jupiter; both hands Shikhara, left held at left shoulder, right held at right side of waist, to indicate the sacred thread. *Shukra:* Venus; left, Mushti, high up, and right, Mushti, down. *Shani:* Saturn; left, Shikhara, right, Trishula. *Rahu:* Left, Sarpashirsha and right, Suchi. *Ketu:* left, Suchi and right, Pataka.

NAVARASA (*Navarasa*): The nine sentiments or rasas. See *Rasa*.

NAYAKA (*Nāyaka*): Romantic hero. Term also loosely includes *Upapati* or lover and *Vaishikha* or libertine. Generally of high birth, possessing beauty, grace, talent, and sometimes divine traits. May be of four kinds, namely: *Anukoola:* (a husband), *Dakshina* (one whose affection is distributed), *Drishta* (one who is always guilty but asks for forgiveness), *Shatha* (one who is mean, crafty and treacherous in love). A further classification is thus: *Dheerodatta* (strong, compassionate and intelligent), *Dheerodhatta* (proud, intolerant, hot-tempered, domineering and a wastrel), *Dheeralalita* (carefree and pleasure-loving), *Dheerashanta* (serene, cheerful and self-reliant).

NAYIKA (*Nāyikā*): Heroine, the romantic concept of the beloved. The different types of Nayikas are described in *Bhavaprakasham*, *Rasa Manjari* and other Sanskrit treatises. Most writers consider 384 types. According to Dharma, nayikas are divided into three main classes. They are: *Sweeya:* (one's wife; also called *Swakeeya*), *Parakeeya:* (nayika who is another's wife), *Sadharana* or *Samanya:* (a common harlot).

Sweeya, a chaste and devoted wife can be classified as: *Mugdha:* (at the very inception of youth and love), *Madhya:* (who is full of youth and love), *Pragalbha:* (who is blind with love).

Madhya and *Pragalbha* nayikas are further categorised thus: *Dheera:* (whose lover is at fault and hence she is sarcastic in speech, making him unhappy), *Adheera:* (whose lover is at fault and she uses harsh words), *Dheeradheera:* (whose lover is at fault and hence she cries and scolds him at the same time); and again as: *Jyeshta:* (the elder wife), *Kanishta:* (the younger wife and hence the favourite). Thus Sweeya Nayikas are thirteen, i.e. one Mugdha, six Madhya, six Pragalbha.

Parakeeya Nayikas are of two types, namely *Udha* (married), *Anudha* (unmarried).

Samanya Nayika is of only one kind. Thus in all, nayikas are fundamentally divided into these 16 types; each of these can be further divided into one of eight categories. (Thus there are 128 categories of Nayikas.) These are called *ashta nayikas*, and may be enumerated thus: *Abhisarika:* (Nayika who goes with intense love to meet her lover, or makes him come to her, in spite of impediments). *Kalahantarita:* (Nayika who first rejects her lover angrily and then repents). *Khandita:* (Nayika who knows that her lover had gone to another woman and is therefore jealous and angry with him). *Proshitapatika:* (Nayika whose lover has gone away on business. Also *Proshitapriya*). *Swadheenapatika:* (Nayika who is assured of the love and the services of her lover. Also *Swadheenabhartrika*). *Vasakasajjita:* (Nayika who adorns herself before she received her lover). *Vipralabdha:* (Nayika who is disappointed or deceived by her lover who fails to meet her at the appointed place and time). *Virahotkantita:* (Nayika who is disturbed by the absence of her innocent lover). Nayikas are also classified into 3 types, depending on their culture and upbringing: *Uttama:* (who returns good for evil and is always happy in her husband's happiness), *Madhyama:* (whose lover is angry and hence she also becomes angry. If the lover is good she is also good to him), *Adhama:* (who is characterless, angry, quarrelsome and jealous). Thus there are 384 Nayikas.

NIDRA (*Nidrā*) [NS]: Vyabhichari bhava of sleep; Vibhavas—weakness, fatigue, intoxication, indolence, thinking too much, over-eating, drowsiness, etc.; anubhavas—heaviness, rolling of the body or the eyes, yawning, massaging the body, breathing deeply, relaxing, closing the eyes, etc.

NIHANCHITA (*Nihañcita*) [NS]: Shiro bheda; the shoulders are raised and the head is bent to one side. Denotes a proud woman, amorousness, light-heartedness, affected indifference, hysteria, slight expression of affection, pretended anger, paralysis, jealousy, anger.

NIKUNCHITA (*Nikuñcita*) [NS]: See *Karana*.

NIKUTTAKA (*Nikuṭṭaka*) [NS]: See *Karana*.

NIMESHA (*Nimeṣa*) [NS]: Puta chalana; the eyelids are closed. Denotes anger.

NIMILITA (*Nimilita*) [AD]: Drishti bheda; half-closed eyes. Denotes a snake, being under another man's power, praying, meditating, salutations, lunacy, observing keenly.

NIRBHUGNA (*Nirbhugna*) [NS]: Hridaya krama; the chest is held stiff and straight, back depressed, shoulders raised and unbent. Denotes paralysis, resentment, surprise, assertion of truth, haughtiness, pride, etc.

——— [NS]: Mukha bheda; mouth is lowered. Denotes looking into a depth, etc.

NIRVEDA (*Nirveda*) [NS]: Vyabhichari bhava of discouragement; vibhavas—poverty, being insulted or abused, being beaten, loss of loved ones, knowledge of Ultimate Truth, etc.; anubhavas—sighing, breathing deeply, deliberation, etc.

NISHADHA (*Niṣadha*) [NS]: Samyuta hasta; left hand in Mushti is placed on right arm above elbow and the right hand is placed on the left arm similarly. Denotes patience, intoxication, pride, elegance, eagerness, valour, arrogance, conceit, haughtiness, motionlessness, steadiness, etc.

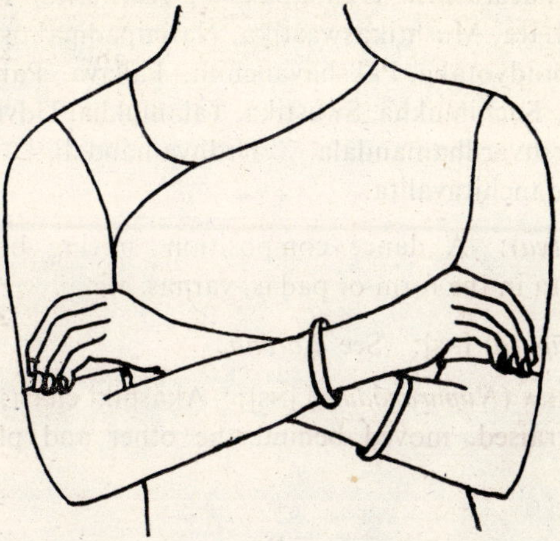

Nishadha

NISHKRAMANA (*Niṣkramaṇa*) [NS]: Tara bheda; the eyeballs are moved outwards; used in depiction of adbhuta rasa.

NISHUMBHITA (*Niśumbhita*) [NS]: See *Karana*.

NITAMBA (*Nitamba*) [NS]: See *Karana*.

——— [NS]: Nritta hasta; two Pataka hands are moved away from the shoulders and placed on the hips.

NIVESHA (*Niveṣa*) [NS]: See *Karana*.

NIVRITTA (*Nivṛtta*) [NS]: Kati krama; from the reverse position the waist is turned to the front; used when turning round in a dance sequence.

NRITTA (*Nṛtta*): Pure dance having no theme and containing adavus, rhythm patterns, poses and adavu jatis, such as jatiswaras, thillanas, alarippus, etc.

NRITTA HASTA (*Nṛtta Hasta*) [AD, NS]: Hastas used in performing nritta and adavus. AD mentions the following asamyuta and samyuta hastas for inclusion in this category: Alapadma, Anjali, Dola, Hamsasya, Kapittha, Katakavardhamana, Kilaka, Kurma, Pasha, Pataka, Shakata, Shikhara, Swastika. Ardhapataka, Chatura, Katakamukha and Tripataka are also included. NS mentions 28 hastas and dynamic movements, viz., Alapallava, Aralakatakamukha, Ardharechita, Aviddhavaktraka, Chaturashra, Dandapaksha, Karihasta, Keshabandha, Lalita, Lata, Mushtikaswastika, Nalinipadmakosha, Nitamba, Pakshapradyotaka, Pakshavanchita, Pallava, Parshvamandali, Rechita, Suchimukha, Swastika, Talamukha, Udvritta, Ulbana, Urahparshvardhamandala, Urdhvamandali, Uromandali, Uttanamanchitavalita.

NRITYA (*Nṛtya*): A dance composition having both abhinaya and nritta in the form of padas, varnas, etc.

NUPURA (*Nūpura*) [NS]: See *Karana*.

NUPURAPADIKA (*Nūpurapādika*) [NS]: Akashiki chari; one Anchita foot is raised, moved behind the other and placed on the ground.

P

PADA (*Pada*): Devotional songs; sometimes expressing shringara rasa; structurally similar to other musical compositions having pallavi, anupallavi and charanas and containing the composer's ankita nama. Shringara padas contain nayaka-nayika lakshanas or references to the love episodes of the patron king. Purandaradasa and Vyasarayaswamy are the earliest and most famous composers of devotional padas while Kshetrangna is considered king of the composers of shringara padas. His compositions in Telugu deal with the amorous deeds of Krishna and contain his ankita nama 'Muvva Gopala'.

PADA KRAMA (*Pāda Krama*) [NS]: Movements of the feet; 5 of these—Agratalasanchara, Anchita, Kunchita, Sama, Udghatita.

PADAPAVIDDHAKA (*Pādapāviddhaka*) [NS]: See *Karana*.

PADARECHAKA (*Pādarecaka*): Rechaka; moving feet from side to side with wavering steps or each foot moving differently.

PADARTHABHINAYA (*Padārthābhinaya*): Abhinaya rendered according to the meaning of the words of the pada.

PADA VARNA (*Pada Varṇa*): Chauka varna; shringara rasa composition or composition in praise of a god or king. See *Varna*.

PADMAKOSHA (*Padmakoṣa*) [AD, NS]: Asamyuta hasta; fingers separated and bent making the palm hollow. Denotes (AD) fruits, a ball, cooking vessel, breasts, a circular movement, eating, bud, mango, scattering flowers, cluster of flowers, bell, ant-hill, lotus, egg; and (NS) bilva and Kapittha fruits, breasts, offering worship, carrying a casket, offering the first funeral cake, flowers.

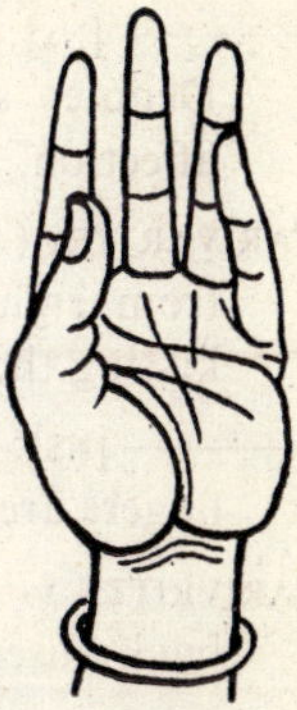

Padmakosha

PAKSHAPRADYOTAKA (*Pakṣapradyotaka*) [NS]: Nritta hasta; Pakshavanchita hands are turned round.

PAKSHAVANCHITA (*Pakṣavañcita*) [NS]: Nritta hasta; two Tripataka hands are placed at either side of the waist.

PALLAVA (*Pallava*) [NS]: Nritta hasta; Pataka hands crossed at the wrists.

PALLAVI (*Pallavī*): First line in a musical composition sung many times in various ways conforming to the raga; followed by anupallavi and charanas after which pallavi is sung again.

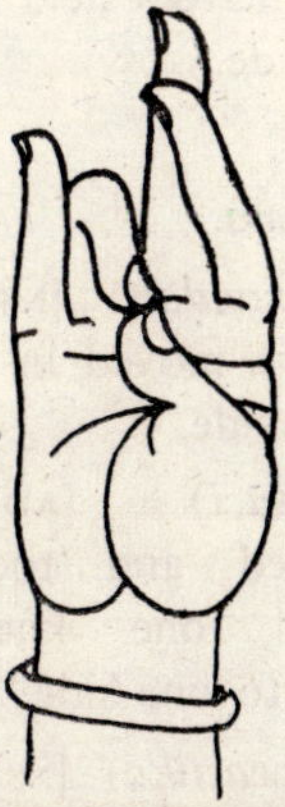

Palli

PALLI (*Pallī*) [AD]: One of the four extra asamyuta hastas; the middle finger of Mayura is placed on the back of the fore-finger. Denotes a village or hut.

PANCHAKRIYA (*Pañcakriyā*): Five kriyas of Nataraja, viz., srishti, sthiti, laya, tiro-bhava, anugraha. See *Nadanta*.

PARACHHINNA (*Parachinna*) [NS]: See *Angahara*.

PARAKEEYA NAYIKA (*Parakīya Nāyikā*): Nayika who is not one's wife; may be further classified as mugdha, madhya or pragalbha or jyeshta or kanishta.

PARAVRITTA (*Parāvṛtta*) [NS]: See *Angahara*.

———: [AD, NS]: Shiro bheda; the head is turned round. Denotes (AD), anger, shame, a slight, turning the face away, hair, quiver, etc., and (NS), turning the face away, looking back, etc.

PARIVAHITA (*Parivāhita*) [AD]: Shiro bheda; addami movement. Denotes infatuation, yearning, uttering praises of god, satisfaction, approval.

——— [NS]: Shiro bheda; the head is moved from side to side. Denotes surprise, joy, remembering, intolerance, cogitation, affection, amorous sport, etc.

PARIVARTITA (*Parivartiṭa*) [NS]: Greeva bheda; the neck is moved from right to left like a half moon. Denotes hasya rasa, kissing the beloved's cheeks.

——— [NS]: Hasta karana; beginning with the little finger the fingers are gradually pointed outward and moved round.

PARIVRITTA (*Parivṛtta*) [NS]: Jangha krama; the shank is turned back; used in various dance sequences.

——— : See *Karana*.

PARIVRITTAKARECHITA (*Parivṛttakarecita*) [NS]: See *Angahara*.

PARSHVACHHEDA (*Pārṣvacheḍa*) [NS]: See *Angahara*.

PARSHVAJANU (*Pārṣvajānu*) [NS]: See *Karana*.

PARSHVA KRAMA (*Pārṣva Krama*) [NS]: Movements of the sides; 5 of these—Apasarpita, Nata, Prasarita, Unnata, Vivartita.

PARSHVAKRANTA (*Pārṣvakrānta*): Akashiki chari, one foot held in Kunchita, the other lifted and brought to one side.

——— [NS]: See *Karana*.

PARSHVANIKUTTITA (*Pārṣvanikuṭṭita*) [NS]: See *Karana*.

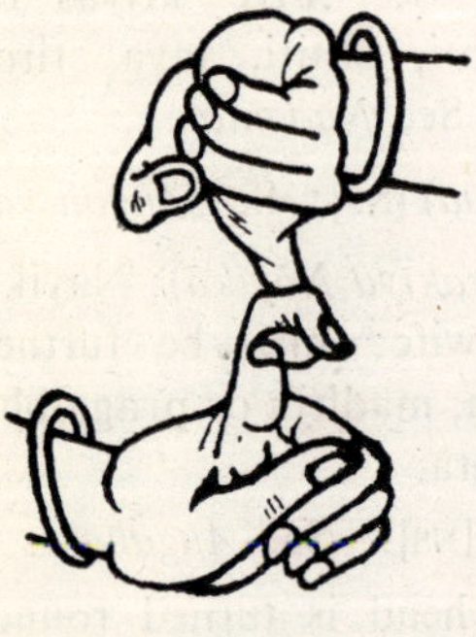

Pasha

PARSHVAMANDALI (*Pārṣvamaṇḍalī*) [NS]: Nritta hasta; hands are moved in a circular fashion to one side.

PARSHVASUCHI (*Pārṣvasūci*) [AD]: Mandala; heels raised and toes touching the ground, one knee placed on the ground to one side.

PARSHVASWASTIKA (*Pārṣvaswastika*) [NS]: See *Angahara*.

PARYASHTAKA (*Paryaṣṭaka*) [NS]: See *Angahara*.

PASHA (*Pāṣa*) [AD]: Samyuta hasta, forefingers of Suchi hands are interlocked. Denotes, a quarrel, string, enemy, chain.

PATAKA (*Patāka*) [AD, NS]: Asamyuta hasta, all the fingers joined and stretched, thumb bent and held at the base of the fore-finger. Denotes (AD) the beginning of a dance, clouds, a forest, forbidding, bosom, might, a river, heaven, a horse, cutting, wind, lying down, going, prowess, favour, moonlight, strong sunlight, opening a door, number seven, case-endings, a wave, entering a street, equality, anointing, taking an oath, silence, palmyra leaf, a shield, touching things, benediction, the ideal king, referring to a place, the sea, good deeds, addressing a person, going forward, holding a sword, a month, a year, a rainy day, sweeping; and (NS) hitting, heat, urging, attaining happiness, arrogant reference to oneself, glare (of the sun), heavy rain, a bower, a shallow pool, flowers, grass, rangoli or kolam, closing or opening something, protecting, covering, dense, private, movements of wind, waves, flood, encouragement, saying 'many', a crowd, height, beating a drum, flight of birds, anything washed, pressed, cleaned or pounded, holding up or uprooting a hill.

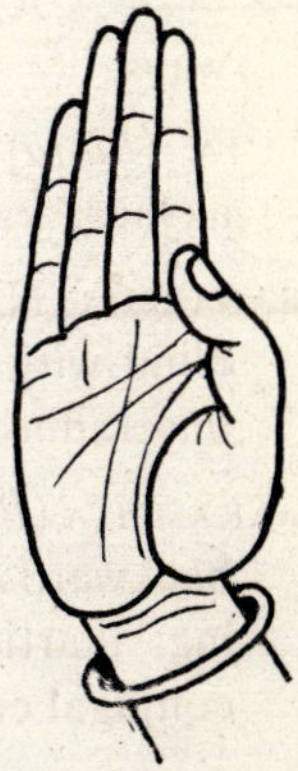

Pataka

PATANA (*Patana*) [NS]: Bhru chalana; the eyebrows are lowered simultaneously or one by one. Denotes envy, disgust, a smile, the act of smelling something.

——— [NS]: Tara bheda; the eyeballs are relaxed. Used in depicting karuna rasa.

PATRA DOSHA (*Pātra Doṣa*): Disqualifications in the appearance of a dancer or danseuse, e.g. obesity or thinness, scanty hair or baldness, poor posture or other disabilities, a squint, bad voice, etc.

PATRA LAKSHANA (*Pātra Lakṣaṇa*): Qualifications for a dancer or danseuse, e.g., youth, well-proportioned, firm, supple body, good personality, skill in all aspects of natya, good birth, good voice, and beautiful face and eyes.

PEEHITA (*Pīhita*) [NS]: Puta chalana; eyelids are at rest. Denotes dreaming, fainting, affliction owing to a storm, smoke, rain or disease.

PHULLA (*Phulla*) [NS]: Ganda krama; cheeks are blown or raised. Denotes joy.

PLAVANA (*Plavana*) [AD]: See *Utplavana*.

——— : Adavu; jumping in different directions and in different ways.

PLUTA (*Pluṭa*): Tala-anga corresponding to 3 laghus or 12 akshara kalas. See *Tala*.

PRAGALBHA NAYIKA (*Pragalbha Nāyikā*) [NS]: Nayika who is blind with love; may be further classified as dheera, adheera, dheeradheera or as jyeshta and kanishta. See *Nayika*.

PRAKAMPITA (*Prakampita*) [AD]: Greeva bheda; the neck is moved backwards and forwards. Denotes saying 'you and I', swinging, inarticulate murmurings, sounds uttered by women in conjugal embrace. Also used in folk dance sequences.

——— [NS]: Hridaya krama; chest is heaved and shaken. Denotes laughing, weeping, weariness, pain, asthma, hiccoughing, misery.

——— [NS]: Kati krama, the waist is moved up and down or obliquely. Denotes a hunchback or a person of the inferior type walking.

PRAKRITA (*Prakṛta*) [NS]: Tara bheda; eyeballs held in their natural state.

PRALAYA (*Pralaya*) [NS]: Śatvika bhava of fainting; vibhavas—overwork, shock, intoxication, sleep, an injury, etc.

PRALOKITA (*Pralokita*) [AD]: Drishti bheda; looking from side to side. Denotes looking at things situated at either side of one, great affection, moving, idiocy.

PRASANNA (*Prasanna*) [NS]: Mukha raga; bright face, denoting wonder, laughter, love.

PRASARITA (*Prasārita*) [NS]: Parshva krama; the sides are stretched out. Denotes joy.

——— [NS]: Puta chalana; eyelids are separated and eyes opened wide. Denotes wonder, joy, heroism.

PRASARPITA (*Prasarpita*) [NS]: See *Karana*.

PRASHTASWASTIKA (*Praṣṭaswastika*) [NS]: See *Karana*.

PRATYALIDHA (*Pratyālidha*) [AD]: Mandala; the hands and feet in Alidha are interchanged.

——— [NS]: Sthanaka; right foot is bent, and left is placed forward. Denotes getting weapons ready for battle.

PRATYANGA (*Pratyaṅga*): Angikabhinaya; abhinaya involving movements of the shoulder blades, arms, back, belly, thighs (and calves) and shanks.

PRENKHANA (*Preṅkhana*) [AD]: Mandala; hands held Kurma, one foot placed next to the heel of the other.

PRENKHOLITA (*Preṅkholita*) [NS]: See *Karana*.

PRERITA (*Prerita*) [AD]: Mandala; one foot kept one and a half cubits away from the other, then one knee kept across the other, Shikhara hands at chest, then stretched out as Pataka.

PROSHITABHARTRIKA (*Prośitabhartrika*): Nayika whose lover had gone away on some work. Also called Proshitapriya.

PROSHITAPATRIKA (*Prośitapatrika*): Nayika assured of the love and services of her lover. Also called Swadheenapatika.

PROSHITAPRIYA (*Prośitapriya*): See *Proshitabhartrika*.

PURNA (*Purṇa*) [NS]: Ganda krama; cheeks are expanded fully, denotes energy, arrogance.

PURVA RANGA (*Pūrva Raṅga*): Preliminaries to a natya performance, described in the fifth chapter of *Natya Shastra*. Before the opening of the curtain, music is played on stringed instruments to the accompaniment of percussion, followed by the recitation of verses and songs.

PUSHPANJALI (*Puṣpāñjali*): Offering of flowers to god before a performance, usually woven into a short dance sequence.

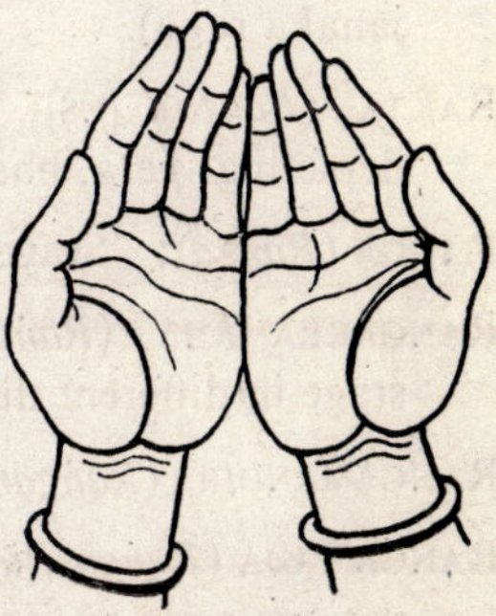

Pushpaputa

PUSHPAPUTA (*Puṣpapūṭa*) [AD, NS]: Samyuta hasta; two Sarpashirsha hands meet at the sides, little fingers touching, palms facing upwards. Denotes (AD) arati, adoration, taking water, fruit, giving offerings to gods, evening, a magic flower; and (NS) receiving or carrying rice, fruit, flowers and other food, carrying and removing water.

PUTA CHALANA (*Puṭa Çālana*) [NS]: Movements of eyelids; 9 of these—Kunchita, Nimesa, Pasarita, Peehita, Sama, Sphurita, Unmesha, Vitadita, Vivartita.

R

RAGA (*Rāga*): Musical mode; a set of swaras from the musical octave. Traditionally considered to have four characteristics —varna (the desire to sing), aroha (arohana—ascending notes), avaroha (avarohana—descending notes) and sanchari (a combination of the preceding two). Ragas are chosen in natya to depict bhava and rasa. Janaka ragas, the melakarta ragas, are 72 in number; these use all the seven notes and are therefore called sampoorna ragas. From these are derived, by the omission of notes, the janya ragas. Janya ragas are classified as: Audhava (five notes in both aroha and avaroha), and Shadava (six notes in both aroha and avaroha), and combinations of these, viz. audhava-shadava, shadava-audhava, audhava-sampurna, shadava-sampurna, sampurna-audhava, sampurna-shadava.

A further classification delineates upanga ragas (janya ragas with the same swara structure as the janaka raga) and bhashanga ragas (janya ragas with 1, 2 or 3 swaras different from the janaka raga).

RAKTA (*Rakta*) [NS]: Mukha raga; reddened face. Used in depicting veera, bhayanaka, raudra and karuna rasas.

RANGA (*Raṅga*): Stage.

RANGAKRAMANA (*Raṅgakramaṇa*): Adavu; moving across the stage in different directions.

RANGAMANDIRA (*Raṅgamandira*): Theatre.

RANGA PUJA (*Raṅga Pūja*): Offering worship to the stage and the various gods on it; detailed description of this is given in the third chapter of *Natya Shastra*. Nowadays performed by giving arati and pushpanjali.

RANGAPRAVESHA (*Raṅgapraveṣa*): See *Arangetram*.

Adbhuta

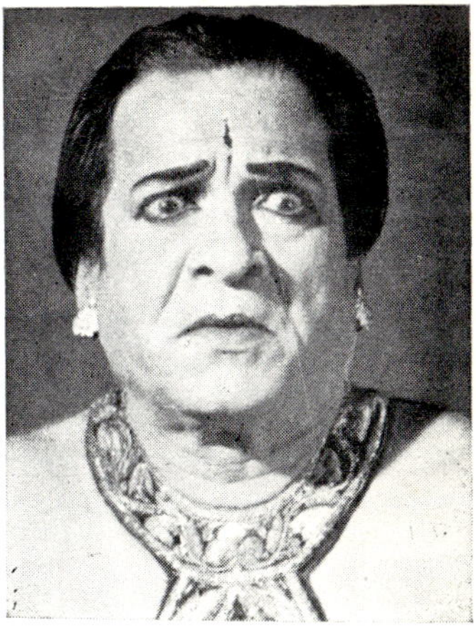

Bhayanaka

Bibhatsa

Hasya

Karuna

Raudra

Shringara

Veera

Shanta

RASA (*Rasa*): Sentiment; produced by the combination of vibhavas, anubhavas and vyabhichari bhavas or by the interaction of sthayi, vyabhichari and satvika bhavas. NS mentions 8 rasas, viz., adbhuta, bhayanaka, bibhatsa, hasya, karuna, raudra, shringara, veera. Modern usage includes a ninth, viz. shanta.

Ashta Rasa: The 8 rasas dealt with in NS.

Nava Rasa: The 9 rasas as in modern usage.

RATI (*Ratī*) [NS]: Sthayi bhava of love; gives rise to shringara rasa. Vibhavas—the seasons, flowers, perfumes, ornaments, the presence of the loved one; anubhavas—sweet words and smiles, movement of the eyebrows.

RAUDRA RASA (*Raudra Rasa*): Rasa of fury, presiding deity—Rudra, sthayi bhava—krodha, representative colour—red. Vibhavas—anger, rape, abuse, insult, untrue allegations, threats, desire for revenge, jealousy, etc.; anubhavas—red eyes, knitted brows, defiant attitude, biting the lips, movement of the cheeks, pressing one hand against the other, etc.; Vyabhichari bhavas—presence of mind, energy, determination, indignation, restlessness, fury, perspiration, trembling, horripilation, choked voice, etc.

RECHAKA (*Recaka*) [NS]: Movements of any limb in a circular manner and distinct from karanas, charis, etc. Four of these, viz., greeva, hasta, kati and pada rechakas.

RECHAKANIKUTTITA (*Recakanikuṭṭita*) [NS]: See *Angahara*.

——— [NS]: Bhru chalana; one eyebrow is raised. Used in the depiction of shringara rasa.

——— [NS]: Greeva bheda; the neck is shaken; Denotes emotion, churning.

——— [NS]: Kati krama; the waist is moved in all directions. Used in several dance movements.

——— [NS]: Nritta hasta; Hamsapaksha hands, palms facing upwards, are moved swiftly.

ROMANCHA (*Romāñca*) [NS]: Satvika bhava of horripilation. Vibhaf vas—touch of a loved one, cold, joy, fever, anger, illness.

RUPAKA TALA (*Rūpaka Tāla*): Tala having one anudruta and one laghu. See *Tala*.

S

Sabha (*Sabhā*): Audience.

Sabhapati (*Sabhāpati*): President of the audience or assembly, traditionally having the qualities of intelligence, discrimination, judgement, ability to speak many languages and skilled in music and other arts. He should also be wealthy, generous, honest, pious, decorous, above malice or envy, and above all, capable of commanding an audience.

Sachi (*Sāci*) [AD]: Drishti bheda; a sidelong glance. Denotes hurting, touching the moustache, hitting a target with an arrow, a parrot, remembering, beginning something.

Sadharana Nayika (*Sādhāraṇa Nāyikā*): A common harlot. Also called Samanya nayika.

Sahaja (*Sahaja*) [NS]: Bhru chalana; eyebrows held naturally.

Sama (*Sama*): The natural position.

——— [NS]: Chibuka krama; lips held slightly apart as in the natural position.

——— [AD]: Drishti bheda; looking straight ahead. Denotes the beginning of natya, scale, effort to read another's mind, surprise, the image of god.

——— [NS]: Ganda krama; cheeks held naturally.

——— [NS]: Greeva bheda; neck held naturally denoting meditation, praying.

——— [NS]: Hridaya krama; chest held naturally, limbs in Chaturashra, body in Saushthava.

——— [NS]: Pada krama; feet placed on even ground, natural position.

——— [NS]: Puta chalana; natural position of eyelids; used to show love.

——— [AD, NS]: Shiro bheda; head held motionless and straight; used in beginning of nritya, praying, to denote pride, stupefaction, etc.

Samabhanga (*Samabhaṅga*): Bhanga; the body is held straight, weight evenly distributed on both feet which are held close to each other. Depicts devotees, performing penance, etc.

Samanakha (*Samānakha*) [NS]: See *Karana*.

SAMANYA NAYIKA (*Sāmānya Nāyikā*): See *Sadharana Nayika.*

SAMAPADA (*Samapāda*) [NS]: Bhaumi chari, feet held close together, with nails meeting.

——— [AD]: Sthanaka; standing with feet together. Used in depicting offering flowers to gods, playing the role of gods, etc.

——— [NS]: Sthanaka; standing with feet one tala apart, body upright. Used to denote accepting blessings from brahmins, imitating birds, bridegroom during the marriage ceremony, persons in the sky, persons practising vows.

SAMASUCHI (*Samasūci*) [AD]: Mandala; toes and knees are touched to the ground.

SAMBHRANTA (*Sambhrānta*) [NS]: See *Karana.*

SAMDAMSHA (*Samdamṣa*) [AD]: Asamyuta hasta; Padmakosha fingers are brought together and separated repeatedly. Denotes belly, presenting offerings to the gods, a wound, a worm, great fear, worship, the number 5.

Samdamsha (AD)

——— [NS]: the forefinger and thumb of Arala are joined and the palm slightly hollowed. May be held agraja (in front), mukhaja (near the face), or parshvaja (at the side). Denotes plucking flowers, making garlands, taking up grass or hairs or a lamp wick or stick, filling a vessel, upbraiding someone, anger, strong thread, piercing a hole, a bowstring, firmness, arrow, meditation, a small quantity, softness, abuse, envoy, painting, applying collyrium, stem, deliberation, drawing patralekha, a woman squeezing lac-dye.

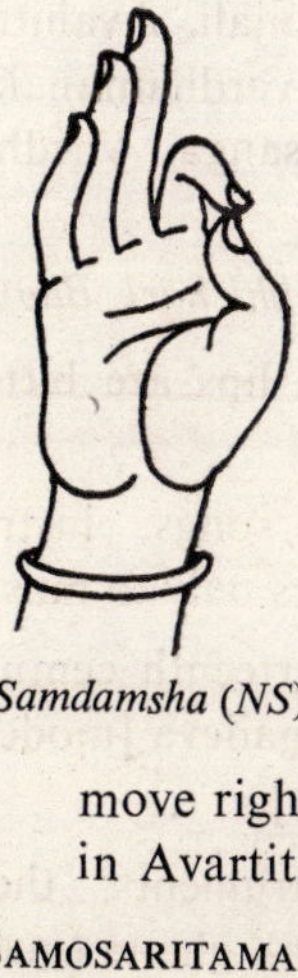

Samdamsha (NS)

SAMOSARITA (*Samosarita*) [NS]: Bhaumi mandala; in Samapada sthanaka stretch out the hands, palms turned upwards; then do Aveshtita and Udveshtita and place left hand on waist; move right in Avartita and place on waist; move left hand in Avartita and then move both hands round alternately.

SAMOSARITAMATTALI (*Samosaritamattali*)[NS]: Bhaumi chari; moving backwards with a circular movement, feet in Talasanchara.

SAMPUTA (*Samputa*) [AD]: Samyuta hasta; the fingers of the Chakra hasta are curved in. Denotes a box, covering something.

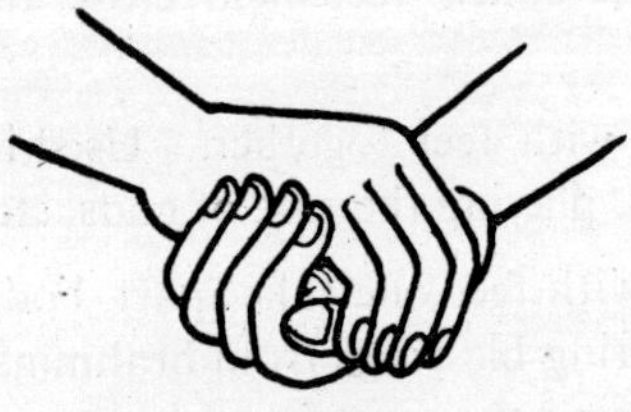

Samputa

SAMPRAVESHANA (*Sampraveśana*) [NS]: Tara bheda; eyeballs are drawn inside; used in depiction of hasya and bhibhatsa rasa.

SAMUDGHATAKA (*Samudghātaka*) [NS]: Adhara krama; contracting the lips and holding them at rest. Denotes pity, kissing, greeting.

SAMUDVRITTA (*Samudvṛtta*) [NS]: Tara bheda; eyelids are raised; used in depiction of veera and raudra rasa.

SAMUNNATA (*Samunnata*): See *Unnata.*

SAMYUTA HASTA (*Samyuṭa Hasta*) [AD, NS]: Representative gestures using both hands. AD mentions 23—Anjali, Bherunda, Chakra, Dola, Garuda, Kapota, Karkata, Kartariswastika, Katakavardhamana, Khatva, Kilaka, Kurma, Matsya, Nagabandha, Pasha, Pushpaputa, Samputa, Shakata, Shankha, Shivalinga, Swastika, Utsanga, Varaha. Some trans. (notably Nidamangalam Tiruvenkatacharya's in Telugu) mention Avahitta, a twenty-fourth. NS mentions 13 — Anjali, Avahitta, Dola, Gajadanta, Kapota, Karkata, Katakavardhamanaka, Makara, Nishada, Pushpaputa, Swastika, Utsanga, Vardhamana.

SANCHARI BHAVA (*Sancāri Bhāva*) [NS]: See *Vyabhichari Bhava.*

SANDASHTAKA (*Sandaṣṭaka*) [NS]: Adhara krama; lips are bitten by the teeth. Denotes anger.

SANGEETA (*Sangīta*): Comprehensive term for songs, instrumental music and dance. Common usage refers only to music.

SANGEETA RATNAKARA (*Sangīta Ratnākara*): Thirteenth century treatise on dance and music written by Sarangadeva [modern edn. Subrahmanya (ed.), Adyar Library, 4 vols].

SANGEETA VADYA (*Sangīta Vādya*): Musical instruments, these being of 4 kinds—avanaddha (covered with skin), ghana (made of solid material), sushira (hollow), tata (stringed).

SANKEERNAJATI (*Sankīrna Jāti*): Laghu containing 9 akshara kalas.

SANNATA (*Sannata*) [NS]: See *Karana*.

SAPTA TALA (*Sapta Tāla*): The seven basic talas are:—Dhruva (1011), Matthya (101), Rupaka (01), Jhampa (1U0), Triputa (100), Atta (1100), and Eka (1). These may be performed in any of the 5 jatis (e.g. Dhruva tala—Tisrajati (11)=$1_3 01_3 1_3$ and Chaturashra jati (14)=$1_4 01_4 1_4$ etc.). Each of these resultant 35 talas may be performed with different gati bhedas of the 5 jatis giving rise totally to 175 talas.

SARANA (*Sarana*) [AD]: Chari; with hands in Pataka, the feet are glided along the ground by joining one heel to the other.

SARANGADEVA (*Sārangadeva*): Author of *Sangeeta Ratnakara*, thirteenth century treatise on dance and music.

SARKAL (*Sarkal*): Adavu. See *Jaru*.

SARPASHIRSHA (*Sarpaśirṣa*) [AD, NS]: Asamyuta hasta; the tips of the fingers of Pataka are curved. Denotes (AD) sandal paste, snake, the middle tone, sprinkling, nourishing, giving water to gods and sages, the movement of the kumbhas (protuberances on the head) of an elephant, arms of wrestlers; and (NS) offering water, pouring water, challenging, movement of an elephant's kumbhas.

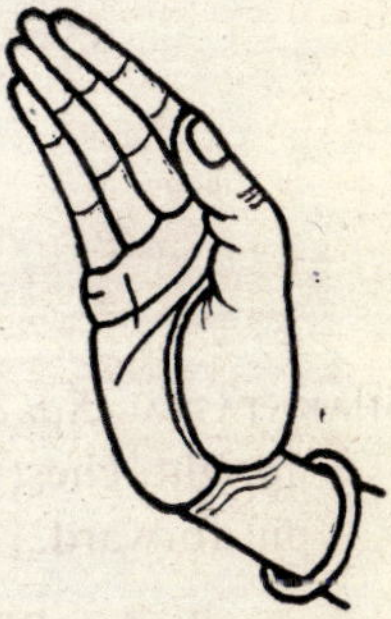

Sarpashirsha

SARPITA (*Sarpita*) [NS]: See *Karana*.

SATVIKABHINAYA (*Sātvikābhinaya*): Abhinaya involving satvika bhavas. See *Chaturvidha Abhinaya*.

SATVIKA BHAVA (*Satvika Bhāva*): Temperamental states caused by concentration of the mind on an emotion; 8 of these—Asra, Kampa, Romancha, Stambha, Swarabheda, Sweda, Vaivarnya, Sausthava.

SAUSTHAVA (*Sausthava*): Position assumed for performing angaharas; the body and limbs should be held relaxed and motionless and in the same positions.

———— : Satvika Bhava.

SHABDAM (*Śabdam*): The first item in a Bharata Natya recital, making use of abhinaya. Previously, called Yashogati (Sanskrit), it is usually in praise of Shiva, Krishna, Muruga or the patron king. Almost all shabdams consist of four lines of literature, sung in Kambodi raga and Misra Chapu tala. Nowadays shabdams are sung in ragamalika starting with Kambodi raga.

SHAKATA (*Śakaṭa*) [AD]: Samyuta hasta; the middle fingers of the two Bhramara hands are stretched out. Denotes a rakshasa.

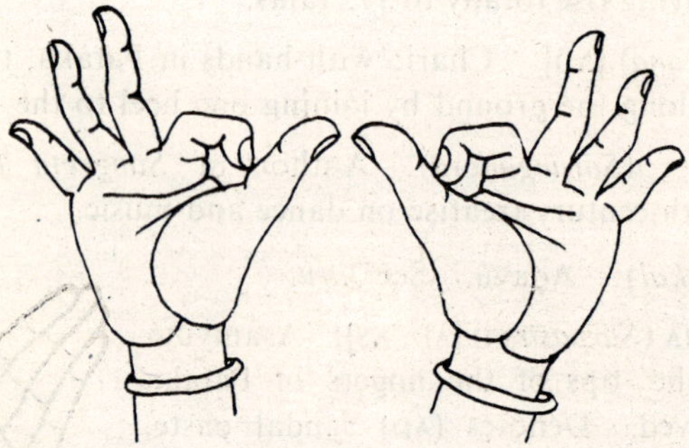

Shakata

SHAKATASYA (*Śakaṭāsya*) [NS]: Bhaumi chari; the body is held upright, chest in Udvahita, and, one Agratalasanchara foot is put forward.

——— [NS]: Bhauma mandala; moving round in this fashion—right foot is moved in Janita chari and then Talasanchara and Shakatasya, left in Syandita chari; the sequence is then repeated with the left leg. This mandala is used when depicting fighting.

——— [NS]: See *Karana*.

SHANKA (*Śaṅkā*) [NS]: Vyabhichari bhava of apprehension, related to women and inferior persons; vibhavas—committing a theft, giving offence to the ruler etc.; anubhavas—fixed state, hesitating movements, dryness of the mouth and licking the lips, change of facial colour, loss of voice, tremors. May arise from one's own acts (depicted by a dark face, thick protruding eyes, tremors, glancing sideways, etc.) or from another's acts (depicted by clever tricks and gestures).

SHANKHA (*Śaṅkha*) [AD]: Samyuta hasta; the thumb of an Ardhachandra hand (left) is clasped by the right Shikhara hand and the fingers of the first are joined to the thumb of Shikhara. Denotes a conch.

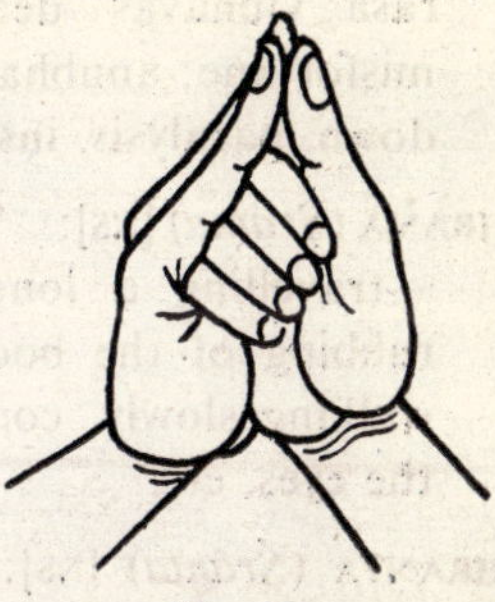

Shankha

SHANKITA (*Śaṅkita*) [NS]: Apprehensive; drishti bheda expressing shanka, vyabhichari bhava of apprehension; the eyes are alternately moved and held steady and are then opened obliquely with a timid expression.

SHANTA RASA (*Śānta Rasa*): The ninth rasa; sentiment of peace; sthayi bhava shama.

Shikhara

SHARIRA (*Śarīra*): Angabhinaya of the limbs. See *Çhaturvidha Abhinaya.*

SHATHA NAYAKA (*Śaṭha Nāyaka*): A nayaka who is mean, crafty and treacherous in love. See *Nayaka.*

SHIKHARA (*Śikhara*) [AD, NS]: Asamyuta hasta; the thumb of mushti is raised. Denotes (AD) armour, bow, pillar, certainty, offerings to the manes, the upper lip, entrance of something, tooth, asking a question, phallic symbol, saying no, recollection, pulling the girdle, embracing, ringing a bell; and (NS) reins, whip, goad, bow, throwing a javelin or spike, painting the lips or feet.

SHIRO BHEDA (*Śiro Bheda*) [AD]: Movements of the head; 9 of these—Adhomukha, Alolita, Dhuta, Kampita, Lolita, Nihanchita, Paravritta, Parivahita, Udvahita, Utkshipta, Vidhuta.

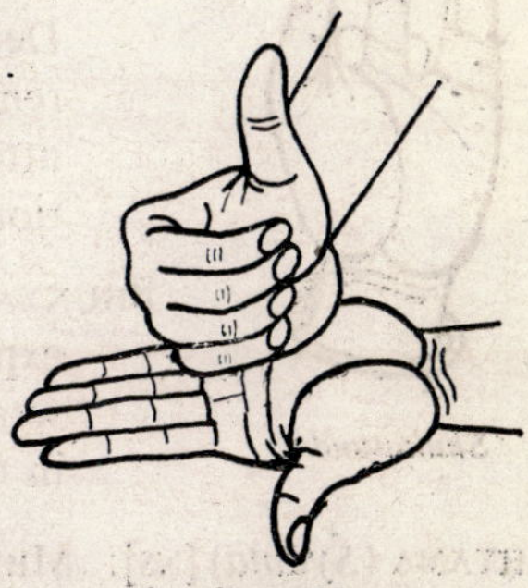

Shivalinga Hasta

SHIVALINGA HASTA (*Śivaliṅga Hasta*) [AD]: Samyuta hasta; right Shikhara hand is placed on left, Ardhachandra. Denotes Shiva, phallic symbol.

SHOKA (*Śoka*) [NS]: Sthayi bhava of sorrow; gives rise to Karuna rasa; vibhavas—death of loved ones, loss of wealth, captivity, misfortune; anubhavas—shedding tears and lamenting, falling down, paralysis, insanity, death.

SHRAMA (*Ṣrama*) [NS]: Vyabhichari bhava of weariness. Vibhavas—travelling a long way, exercise, etc.; anubhavas—gentle rubbing of the body, massaging the limbs, deep breathing, walking slowly, contracting the mouth, belching, contracting the eyes, etc.

SHRANTA (*Śrānta*) [NS]: Tired; drishti bheda expressing vyabhichari bhava. Eyelids droop due to fatigue; the corners of the eyes are narrowed and the eyeballs are lowered.

SHRINGARA RASA (*Ṣṛṅgāra Rasa*): Rasa of love, the most important rasa; presiding deity, Vishnu; sthayi bhava, Rati; representative colour, light green. Vibhavas—the seasons, garlands and unguents, ornaments, the company of the beloved, beautiful gardens, seeing, or dallying with the beloved, sweet words; anubhavas—clever movements of the eyes and eyebrows, quick glances, delicate limb-movements, sweet words. The only vyabhichari bhavas it does not use are fear, indolence, cruelty.

SHRISHTI (*Śṛṣṭi*): Panchakriya of Nataraja; creation as represented by one right hand holding a drum and a deer. See *Nadanta*.

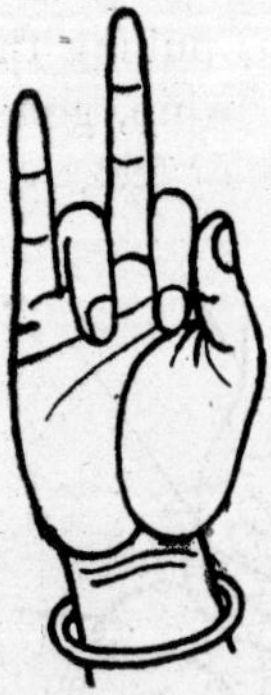

Shukatunda

SHUKATUNDA (*Śukatuṇḍa*) [AD, NS]: Asamyuta hasta; the third finger of Arala is bent or the first finger of Tripataka is bent. Denotes (AD) shooting an arrow, spear, remembering one's abode, mystic utterances, violent mood; and (NS) invocation, saying farewell, upbraiding someone.

SHUNYA (*Śūnya*) [NS]: Vacant; drishti bheda expressing vyabhichari bhava; eyes are weak and motionless, eyelids and eyeballs in the ordinary position, gazing blankly.

SHYAMA (*Śyāma*) [NS]: Mukha raga; dark face. Denotes bhibhatsa and bhayanaka rasa.

SILAPADHIKARAM (*Silapadhikāram*): Tamil epic by Ilango-Adigal containing references to dances and dancing customs of the times. Deals with the tragic love story of Kovalan, his wife Kannaki and the beautiful dancing girl Madhavi: Enticed by Madhavi, Kovalan loses his wealth and goes with Kannaki to Madurai. Trying to sell Kannaki's golden anklet he is accused of theft and executed by the Pandyan king. Kannaki, heartbroken, breaks open the anklet and proves the injustice of Kovalan's punishment. The king dies; Kannaki tears her breast and throws it over Madurai which is then destroyed by fire.

SIMHA GATI (*Simha Gati*) [AD]: Gati bheda; walking like a lion; standing on toes and jumping forward holding Shikhara hands.

SIMHAKARSITA (*Simhakarsita*) [NS]: See *Karana*.

SIMHAMUKHA (*Simhamukha*) [AD]: Asamyuta hasta; tips of the middle and ring fingers are joined to the thumb and the other two fingers are raised and stretched. Denotes a lion's face, homa, hare, elephant, waving kusha grass, lotus garland, deer, cow, preparing medicine, rectifying something.

Simhamukha

SIMHAVIKRIDITA (*Simhavikrīḍita*) [NS]: See *Karana*.

SKHALITA (*Skhalita*) [NS]: See *Karana*.

SMITA (*Smita*): Aspect of hasya rasa; slight smile by the superior type of person.

SMRITI (*Smṛtī*) [NS]: Vyabhichari bhava of recollection. Vibhavas—remembering happiness or sorrow; impaired health, disturbed sleep, seeing and speaking with a level head, thinking, constant practice, etc.; anubhavas—nodding of the head, looking down, raising the eyebrows, etc.

SNIGDHA (*Snigdha*) [NS]: Loving. Drishti bheda expressing sthayi bhava of rati. The eyes are widened slightly and a sweet expression assumed, the eyeballs held still, occasionally with tears of joy.

SOLKATTU (*Solkaṭṭu*): Musical composition having words, and syllables of mridanga jatis and swaras; more often using only the latter, used in singing swarajatis, thillanas, etc., and sung in the same raga as the rest of the composition. Also called sollukattu.

SPHURITA (*Sphurita*) [NS]: Puta chalana, eyelids are made to throb. Depicts jealousy.

STHAMBA (*Sthamba*) [NS]: Satvika bhava of paralysis. Vibhavas—joy, fear, illness, surprise, sorrow, intoxication, anger.

STHAMBANA (*Sthambana*) [NS]: Uru krama; the thighs are held motionless. Denotes despair.

STHANA (*Sthāna*) [NS]: See *Sthanaka.*

STHANAKA (*Sthānaka*) [AD, NS]: Postures assumed at the beginning and end of an adavu. AD mentions 6—Aindra, Brahma, Ekapada, Garuda, Nagabandha, Samapada. NS mentions 6—Alidha, Mandala, Pratyalidha, Samapada, Vaishakha, Vaishnava.

STHAYI BHAVA (*Sthāyi Bhāva*) [NS]: Dominant states of mind caused by vibhavas (cause) and represented by anubhavas (consequents); 8 of these, viz., Bhaya, Hasya, Jugupsa, Krodha, Rati, Shoka, Utsaha, Vismaya.

STHIRAHASTA (*Sthirahasta*) [NS]: See *Angahara.*

STHITAVARTA (*Sthitāvarta*) [NS]: Bhaumi chari; one Agratalasanchara foot is drawn up to cross the other foot; the feet are separated and movement repeated with the other foot.

STHITI (*Sthiti*): Panchakriya of Nataraja; protection or preservation as represented by second right hand in Abhaya hasta. See *Nadanta.*

SUCHASYA (*Sūcasya*) [NS]: Nritta hasta; two Sarpashirsha hands with thumbs touching middle fingers are crossed in Swastika. Also Suchimukha.

——— [NS]: See *Suchi.*

SUCHHVASA (*Sūchvāsa*) [NS]: Nasika krama; inhaling deeply. Denotes fragrance, deep breathing.

SUCHI (*Sūcī*) [NS]: Akashiki chari; one Kunchita foot is raised and brought above the knee of the other leg then dropped on the ground with the heel raised.

——— [NS]: See *Karana.*

——— [AD, NS]: Asamyuta hasta; the forefinger of Kataka-mukha is raised and the other fingers bent into the palm. Denotes (AD) one, Supreme Soul, one hundred, a city, the world, saying thus, threatening, growing thin, rod, body, astonishment, braid, hair, umbrella, capability, beating a drum, potter's wheel, wheel's circumference, considering, decline of day; and (NS) moving sideways, shaking, moving up and down, moving up increasingly, discussing, lighting, banner, blossoms, ear-ring, zig-zag movement, cry of approbation, young serpent, sprout, incense, lamp, creepers, Shikhanda, falling down, a curve or roundness, stars, nose, one, club, stick. Also called Suchasya.

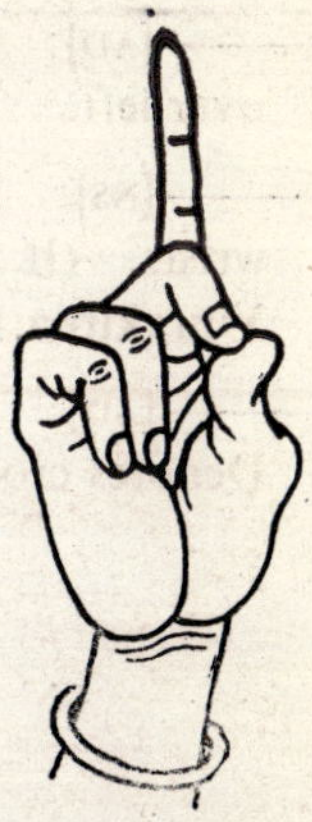

Suchi (AD, NS)

SUCHIMUKHA (*Sūcimukha*) [NS]: See *Suchasya*.

SUCHIVIDDHA (*Sūcividdha*) [NS]: Akashiki mandala; the following charis are performed—left foot in Suchi and Bhramari by turning the trika, right foot in Parshvakranta, left in Atikranta, right in Suchi, left in Apakranta, right in Parshvakranta.

——— [NS]: See *Angahara*.

——— [NS]: See *Karana*.

SUNDARI (*Sundarī*) [AD]: Greeva bheda; the neck is moved horizontally to and fro. Denotes affection, effort, width, approval, pleasure, saying completely. Corresponds to Addami.

SUPTA (*Supta*) [NS]: Vyabhichari bhava of dreaming; vibhavas—interrupted sleep, sense-experience, infatuation, spreading or dragging a bed, etc.; anubhavas—deep breathing, dullness, closing the eyes, stupefaction, etc.

SUSHIRA (*Suśira*): Hollow musical instruments, e.g. flute. See *Sangeeta Vadya*.

SWABHAVIKA (*Swābhāvika*) [NS]: Mukha raga; the natural colour of the face.

——— [NS]: Nasika krama; nostrils held naturally.

SWAKEEYA NAYIKA (*Swakīya Nāyikā*): See *Sweeya Nayika*.

SWASTIKA (*Swastika*): Position where hands or feet are held crossed.

——— [NS]: See *Karana*.

——— [AD]: Mandala; feet and hands crossed in Swastika right over left.

——— [NS]: Nritta hasta; Talamukha hands crossed at the wrists. (If they are separated afterwards the hasta is called Viprakirna.)

——— [AD]: Samyuta hasta; Pataka hands crossed at the wrists. Denotes crocodile.

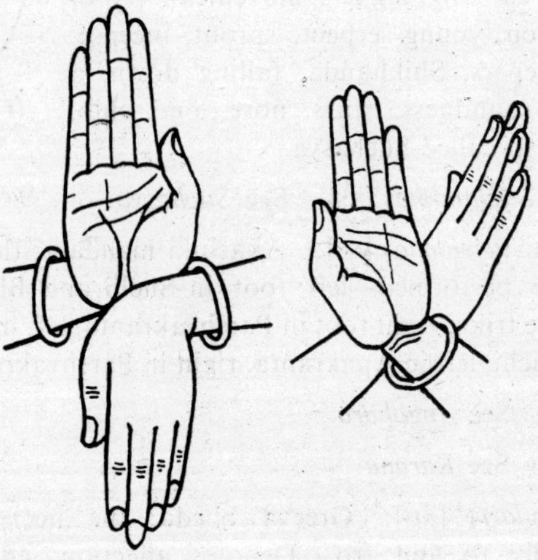

Swastika (AD)

——— [NS]: Samyuta hasta; Arala hands are crossed at the wrists. When the hasta is shown and hands are separated, it denotes directions, clouds, sky, forests, seas, seasons, the earth and other extensive things.

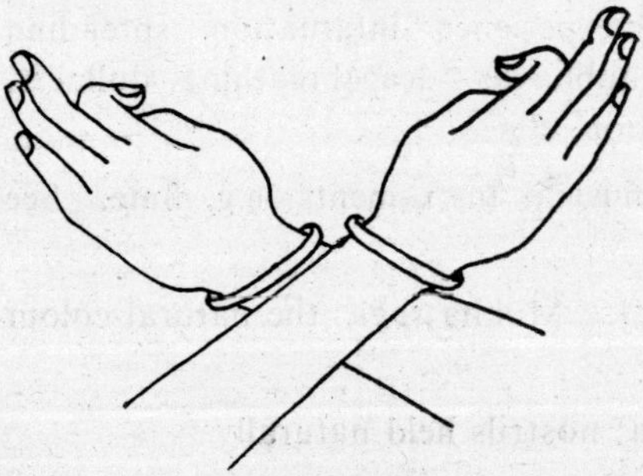

Swastika (NS)

SWASTIKARECHITA (*Swastikarecita*) [NS]: See *Angahara*.

——— [NS]: See *Karana*.

SWADHEENABHARTRIKA (*Swādhīnabhartrikā*): See *Proshitapatrika.*

SWADHEENAPATIKA (*Swādhīnapatikā*): See *Proshitapatrika.*

SWADEENAPATRIKA (*Swādhīnapatrikā*): See *Proshitapatrika.*

SWARA (*Swara*): Musical note. See *Raga.*

SWARA BHEDA (*Swara Bheda*) [NS]: Change of voice. Satvika bhava; Vibhavas—fear, joy, anger, illness, intoxication.

SWARAJATI (*Swarajati*): Musical composition containing solkattu. It also contains the usual pallavi, anupallavi, charanas, swaras and swara sahityas. Usually in praise of Shiva and important in Bharata Natya.

SWEDA (*Sweda*) [NS]: Perspiration; satvika bhava. Vibhavas—anger, fear, joy, sorrow, hard work, illness, heat, fatigue, exercise, massage.

SWEEYA NAYIKA (*Swīya Nāyikā*): Nayika who is also one's wife. May be either mugdha, madhya or pragalbha, further classified as dheera, adheera, and dheeradheera. See *Nayika.*

SYANDITA (*Syāndita*) [NS]: Bhaumi chari; one foot is put forward five talas away from the other.

T

TALA (*Tāla*): Cyclic rhythms. Etymologically derived, according to some authors, from 'ta' (referring to Shiva—the tandava aspect) and 'la' (referring to Parvati—lasya). The union of these two or of the right and left hands produce tala. The smallest of units measured in tala is one akshara kala. Angas of tala are anudruta (one akshara kala; demonstrated by a clap only and represented by U), druta (2 akshara kalas, demonstrated by a clap and a wave and represented by O), laghu (4 akshara kalas or one matra; demonstrated by clapping and counting on the fingers to make up the total number of counts in the particular jati; represented by a vertical line followed by the jati of the laghu, i.e., 1_3, 1_4, etc.), guru, pluta and kakapada (8, 12 and 16 akshara kalas, respectively). The former three are the most commonly used. Laghu changes according to the jatis; these are five in number, namely tryasra (tisra—3 akshara kalas—a clap and 2 counts), chaturashra (chatushra—4 akshara kalas—a clap and 3 counts), khanda (5 akshara kalas—a clap and 4 counts), mishra (7 akshara kalas—a clap and 6 counts) and sankeerna (9 akshara kalas—a clap and 8 counts).

[The 7 basic talas (see also *Sapta Tala*) are Dhruva (1011), Matthya (101), Rupaka (01), Jhampa (1U0), Triputa (100), Atta (1100), Eka (1), and each of these may be in any of the five jatis giving rise to 35 talas, (See page 79)]

——— : A unit of measure; roughly, 1 tala = 30 cm.

TALAMUKHA (*Tālamukha*) [NS]: Nritta hasta; in Chaturashra position, Hamsapaksha hands are held in front at chest level, facing each other.

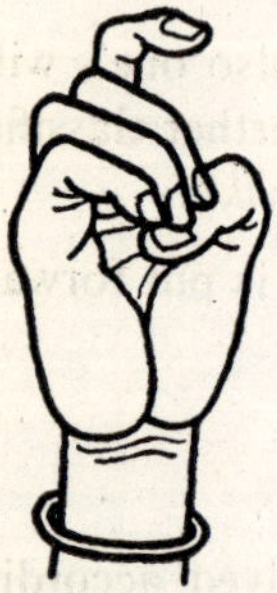

Tamrachuda (*AD*)

TALAPUSHPAPUTA (*Talapuṣpapuṭa*) [NS]: See *Karana*.

TALASAMGHATITA (*Talasamghāṭita*) [NS]: See *Karana*.

TALASAMPOTITA (*Talasampoṭita*) [NS]: See *Karana*.

TALAVILASITA (*Talavilāsita*) [NS]: See *Karana*.

TAMRACHUDA (*Tāmracūḍa*) [AD]: Asamyuta hasta; the forefinger of Mukula is lifted up and curved. Denotes cock, crane, crab, camel, calf, pen.

———[NS]: Asamyuta hasta; the middle finger and thumb are joined to the slightly bent forefinger and the other fingers are bent in. Denotes rebuke, beating time, inspiring confidence, quickness, making a sign, one hundred, one thousand, one lakh, coins, sparks, drops.

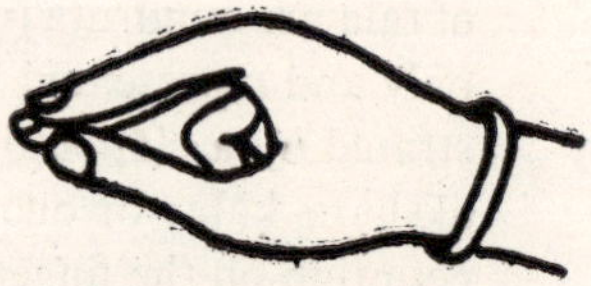

Tamrachuda (*NS*)

TANA VARNA (*Tāna Varṇa*): See *Varna*.

TANDAVA (*Tāṇḍava*): Powerful and virile dance; the opposite of lasya. Originally supposed to have been performed by Tandu (Shiva's attendant) though Shiva is considered the

TALAS

Jatis	Tisra	Chaturashra	Khanda	Mishra	Sankeerna
Dhruva (1011)	1 0 1 1 (11) 3 3 3	1 0 1 1 (14) 4 4 4	1 0 1 1 (17) 5 5 5	1 0 1 1 (23) 7 7 7	1 0 1 1 (29) 9 9 9
Matthya (101)	1 0 1 (8) 3 3	1 0 1 (10) 4 4	1 0 1 (12) 5 5	1 0 1 (16) 7 7	1 0 1 (20) 9 9
Rupaka (01)	01 (5) 3	0 1 (6) 4	0 1 (7) 5	0 1 (9) 7	0 1 (11) 9
Jhampa (1U0)	1 U 0 (6) 3	1 U 0 (7) 4	1 U 0 (8) 5	1 U 0 (10) 7	1 U 0 (12) 9
Triputa (100)	1 0 0 (7) 3	1 0 0 (8) 4 (Aditala)	1 0 0 (9) 5	1 0 0 (11) 7	1 0 0 (13) 9
Atta (1100)	1 1 0 0 (10) 3 3	1 1 0 0 (12) 4 4	1 1 0 0 (14) 5 5	1 1 0 0 (18) 7 7	1 1 0 0 (22) 9 9
Eka (1)	1 (3) 3	1 (4) 4	1 (5) 5	1 (7) 7	1 (9) 9

Each of these can have various gati bhedas (i.e. each beat, wave or finger count may be in any one of the 5 jatis) thus giving rise to 175 talas in all.

supreme master of it. Shaivite literature delineates 7 types of tandava—Ananda (Nadanta, see *Nadanta*), Sandhya (performed in the evening under the banyan tree), Uma (with Uma), Gauri (with Gauri), Kalika (slaying the demons of evil and ignorance), Tripura (slaying the demon Tripura) and Samhara (destruction). Agastya mentions 108 in *Bharata Sutra*, the 12 important ones being Ananda, Sandhya, Shringara, Tripura, Udhva, Muni, Samhara, Urgrava, Bhuta, Pralaya, Bhujanga, Shuddha.

———: Powerful adavu performed by bending the body and legs.

TANDAVA LAKSHANAM (*Tāṇḍava Lakṣaṇam*): Treatise on fundamentals of dance contained in the fourth chapter of *Natya Shastra* and describing the 108 karanas found in the Chidambaram temple. (Trans. Venkata Narayanaswami Naidu, Sreenivasa Naidu and Venkata Rangayya Pantulu.)

TARA BHEDA (*Tāra Bheda*) [NS]: Movements of the eyeballs; 9 of these—Bhramana, Chalana, Nishkramana,Patana, Prakrita, Sampraveshana, Samudvritta, Valana, Vivartana.

TATA (*Taṭa*): Stringed instruments (e.g. veena, violin, etc.). See *Sangeeta Vadya*.

TATTU (*Taṭṭu*): Adavu; stamping feet flat on the ground.

TEERMANAM (*Tīrmānam*): Intricate rhythmic sequence in varnas, sung in any laya by the nattuvanar to the accompaniment of cymbals only. Adavus and jatis are danced to this followed by the repetition of the teermanam on the mridangam.

THILLANA (*Thillāna*): Musical composition used profusely in Bharata Natya. The pallavi and anupallavi use only solkattu and occasionally also swaras. At the end there is usually a short charana in praise of a king or god. Generally performed toward the end of a recital.

TIRASCHHINA (*Tiraschina*) [AD]: Greeva bheda; the neck is moved upwards with a side-to-side movement. Denotes gliding of a snake, fencing.

TIROBHAVA (*Tirobhava*): Panchakriya of Nataraja; illusion as represented by the shrichakra on which the Nadanta icon stands. See *Nadanta*.

TISRA JATI (*Tisra Jāti*): Jati containing 3 akshara kalas.

TRASA (*Trāsa*): Vyabhichari bhava of fear. Vibhavas—lightning, meteors, thunder, earthquake, clouds, cries of wild animals; anubhavas—shaking of the limbs, trembling, paralysis, horripilation, choked voice, talking irrelevantly, etc.

TRASTA (*Trāsta*) [NS]: Drishti bheda expressing trasa, vyabhichari bhava of fear. The eyelids are drawn up, the eyeballs are in tremor and the eyes are opened wide.

TRIBHANGA (*Tribhaṅga*): Bhanga; three-fold bend of the body—at the head, waist and knees. Depicts the stance of goddesses and women and used in lasya dance.

TRIPATAKA (*Tripatāka*) [AD, NS]: Asamyuta hasta; the ring finger of Pataka is bent. Denotes (AD) crown, tree, Indra's vajra, Indra, Ketaki flower, lamp, flames, pigeon, drawing patterns on the face or breast, arrow turning round; and (NS) invocation, descent, bidding someone good-bye, prohibition, entrance, raising something, bowing, comparing, suggesting alternatives, touching an auspicious object, or putting them on the head, wearing a turban or crown, covering the mouth or ears, small birds flying, stream, snake, wiping tears, making tilaka or patralekha, touching one's hair, adoration of venerable person's feet, marriage, king, ascetic, door, planets, submarine, fire, battle, sea-monster, monkey, waves, wind, women, crescent moon, a king marching against the enemy.

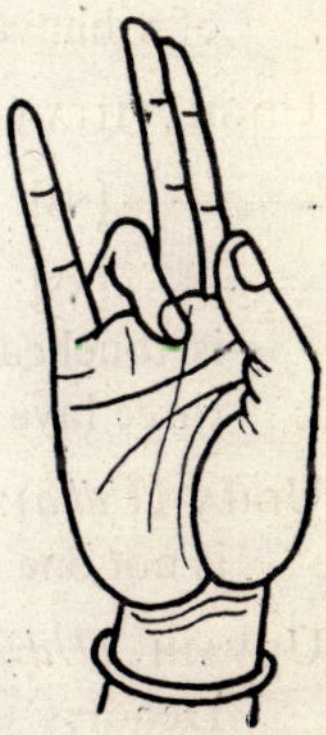
Tripataka

TRIPUTA (*Tripuṭa*): Tala with 1 laghu and 2 drutas.

TRISHULA (*Triṣūla*) [AD]: Asamyuta hasta; the thumb and the little finger are joined and the other three fingers are separated

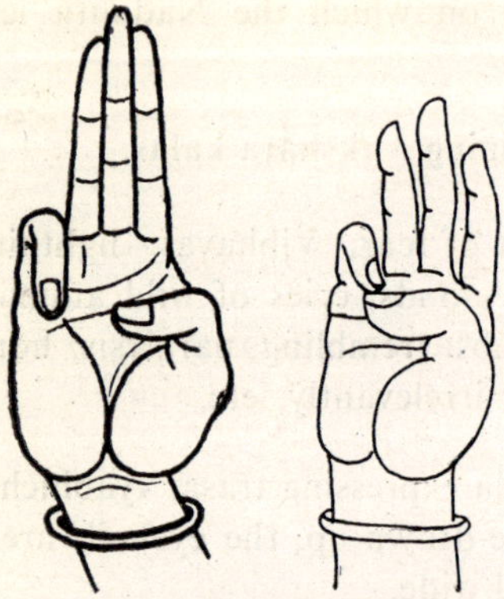

Trishula

and stretched out. Denotes the trident, the Trinity, number 3, betel leaf.

TRYASRA (*Tryasra*) [NS]: Greeva bheda; the neck (and face) is turned sideways. Denotes carrying a weight on the neck.

——— : Tisra Jati.

TURANGA GATI (*Turanga Gati*) [AD]: Gati bheda of the horse; raising each foot (starting with the right) and jumping with right hand Pataka, left Shikhara.

U

UDARA KRAMA (*Udara Krama*) [NS]: See *Jathara Krama*.

UDDIPANA VIBHAVA (*Uddīpana Vibhāva*) [NS]: Secondary cause of a bhava. See *Vibhava*.

UDGHATTITA (*Udghāṭṭita*) [NS]: See *Angahara*.

——— [NS]: See *Karana*.

——— [NS]: Pada krama; after standing on the toes the ground is touched with the heels. Used in Udghattita karana in all three layas.

UDHA (*Udha*): Parakeeya nayika who is married; nayika who is not one's wife and is married (to someone else). See *Nayika*.

UDVAHI (*Udvāhi*) [NS]: Mukha bheda; mouth is turned up. Denotes sportiveness, a proud woman, asking someone to go away, showing disregard, corroborating, speaking angrily.

UDVAHITA (*Udvāhita*) [NS]: Hridaya krama; chest is raised. Denotes breathing deeply, looking at something high up, yawning.

——— [NS]: Jangha krama; the shank is raised. Used in quick walking movements.

——— [NS]: Kati krama; the sides of the waist are raised. Denotes a fat person walking, amorous movement of women.

——— [AD, NS]: Shiro bheda; (AD) the head is raised. Denotes flag, mountain, sky, moon, objects high up, heavenly bodies, etc. and (NS): The head is turned upwards once. Denotes pride, height, looking up, self-esteem, etc.

UDVARTHANA (*Udvarthana*) [NS]: Urukrama; springing up by drawing the knees inward. Used in exercises and nritta sequences.

UDVESHTITA (*Udveṣṭita*) [NS]: Hasta karana; the fingers beginning with the forefinger are pointed outwards and moved around.

UDVRITTA (*Udvṛtta*) [NS]: Akashiki chari; Kunchita foot of Aviddha chari is taken round the other thigh and then placed on the ground.

——— [NS]: See *Karana*.

——— [NS]: Nritta hasta; Hamsapaksha hands are waved like fans.

UDVRITTAKA (*Udvṛttaka*) [NS]: See *Angahara*.

UGRATA (*Ugrata*) [NS]: Vyabhichari bhava of cruelty. Vibhavas—arrest, offence to kings, offensive language, etc.; anubhavas—imprisonment, killing, beating, rebuking, etc.

ULBANA (*Ulbana*) [NS]: Nritta hasta; the hands are stretched up and waved.

ULLOKITA (*Ullokita*) [AD]: Drishti bheda; looking up. Denotes the top of a flag, tower, heavenly bodies, divine birth, height, moonlight.

UNMADA (*Unmada*) [NS]: Vyabhichari bhava of insanity. Vibhavas—death of beloved ones, loss of wealth, injury, derangement of the humours (vata, pittha and kapha); anubhavas—laughing, weeping, crying, talking, lying, sitting, running, dancing, singing, correcting, irrationally smearing ash or dust on the body, plucking grass, nirmalya, soiled clothes, wearing rags, using potsherd or earthen trays as decoration, imitating others, senseless acts.

UNMATTA (*Unmaṭṭa*) [NS]: See *Karana*.

UNMESHA (*Unmeṣa*) [NS]: Puta chalana; the eyelids are separated and the eyes opened wide to show anger.

UNNATA (*Unnata*) [NS]: Greeva bheda; the neck and face are lifted up. Denotes looking upward.

——— [NS]: Parshva krama; Nata is performed and then the other side is raised. Used when moving backwards.

UPAHASITA (*Upahasita*): Aspect of hasya rasa; laughter expressing ridicule; shown by expanded nostrils, squinted eyes and bent head and shoulders.

UPANGA (*Upāṅga*): Abhinaya involving the 12 parts of the head—eyes, eyebrows, eyeballs, cheeks, nose, jaws, lips, teeth, tongue, chin, face, shoulders. See *Chaturvidha Abhinaya*.

UPAPATI (*Upapati*): The lover. See *Nayaka*.

UPASARPITA (*Upasarpita*) [NS]: See *Angahara*.

UPASRITA (*Upasrita*) [NS]: See *Karana*.

URAHPARSHVARDHAMANDALI (*Urahpārṣvārdhamaṇḍali*) [NS]: Nritta hasta; Alapallava and Arala hands are moved alternately above the chest and at the sides.

URDHVAJANU (*Ūrdhvajanū*) [NS]: Akashiki chari; one Kunchita foot is raised to chest level while the other leg is held still; the sequence is repeated with the other leg.

——— [NS]: See *Karana*.

URDHVAMANDALI (*Ūrdhvamandali*) [NS]: Nritta hasta; the hands are moved in a circular manner at shoulder level.

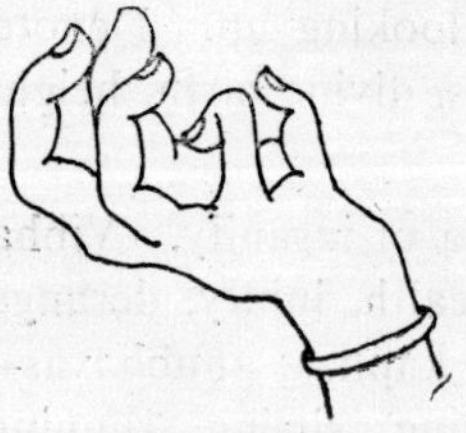
Urnanabha

URNANABHA (*Ūrnanābha*) [NS]: Asamyuta hasta; the fingers of Padmakosha are bent further in. Denotes combing the hair, receiving stolen goods, scratching one's head, skin disease, lions, tigers, picking up a touchstone.

UROMANDALI (*Uromandalī*) [NS]: See *Karana*.

——— [NS]: Nritta hasta; one hand, moving at chest level in a circular manner is raised and the other hung down.

URUDVRITTA (*Urudvṛtta*) [NS]: Akashiki chari; one Kunchita foot of Aviddha chari is moved round the other thigh, raised and placed on the ground.

——— [NS]: Bhaumi chari, the heel of one Talasanchara foot is placed outwards, one of the shanks is bent slightly and the thigh turned up.

——— [NS]: See *Karana*.

URU KRAMA (*Uru Krama*) [NS]: Movements of the thighs; 5 of these—Kampana, Sthambana, Udvartana, Valana, Vivartana.

UTKSHEPA (*Utkṣepa*) [NS]: Bhru chalana; brows are raised simultaneously or one by one. Denotes anger, deliberation, passion, sportiveness, seeing or hearing (one brow), surprise, joy, anger (both brows).

UTKSHIPTA (*Utkṣipta*) [NS]: Shiro bheda; the head is raised slightly. Denotes objects high up, divine things, weapons.

UTPLAVANA (*Utplavana*) [AD]: Ways of jumping; 5 of these—Alaga, Ashva, Kartari, Kripalaga, Motita. Also called plavana.

——— : Adavu: See *Plavana*.

UTPLUTA (*Utpluṭa*) [AD]: Bhramari; moving the body round, starting from Samapada position.

UTSAHA (*Utsāha*) [NS]: Sthayi bhava of energy; gives rise to veera rasa and associated with superior persons. Vibhavas—heroism, patience, power, absence of sorrow; anubhavas—boldness, courage, munificence, steadfastness.

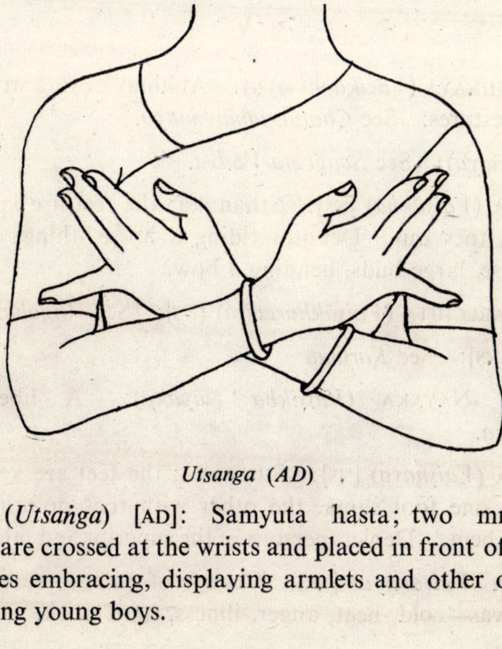

Utsanga (AD)

UTSANGA (*Utsaṅga*) [AD]: Samyuta hasta; two mrigashirsha hands are crossed at the wrists and placed in front of the chest. Denotes embracing, displaying armlets and other ornaments, coaching young boys.

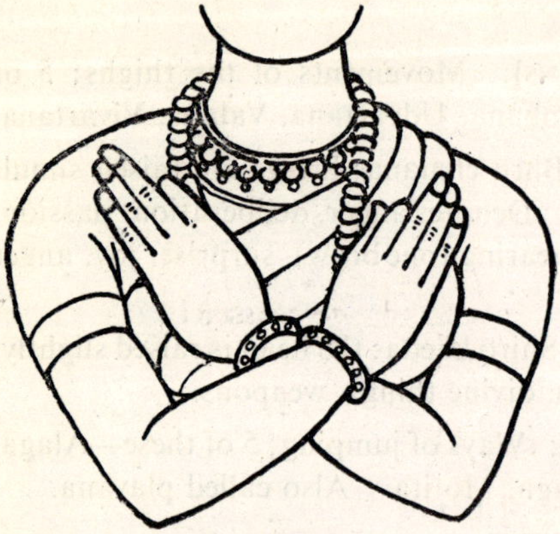

Utsanga (*NS*)

———[NS]: Samyuta hasta; two Arala hands are crossed at the wrists. Denotes touch, effort, acts of anger or indignation, squeezing something, woman's acts of jealousy.

UTSYANDITA (*Utsyandita*) [NS]: Bhaumi chari; the feet are moved sideways (in and out) as in pada rechaka.

UTTAMA NAYIKA (*Uttama Nāyikā*): Woman who returns good for evil and is happy in the happiness of others. See *Nayika*.

UTTANAVANCHITA (*Uttānavañcita*) [NS]: Nritta hasta; Tripataka hands are bent slightly and the shoulders and elbows are moved.

V

VACHIKABHINAYA (*Vācikābhinaya*): Abhinaya using words, speech and gestures. See *Chaturvidhābhinaya*.

VADYA (*Vādya*): See *Sangeeta Vadya*.

VAISHAKHA (*Vaiṣākha*) [NS]: Sthanaka; the feet are kept 3½ talas apart, toes out. Denotes riding a horse, things motionless, exercise, large buds, bending a bow.

VAISHAKHARECHITA (*Vaiṣākharecita*) [NS]: See *Angahara*.

———[NS]: See *Karana*.

VAISHIKHA NAYAKA (*Vaiṣikha Nāyaka*): A libertine. See *Nayaka*.

VAISHNAVA (*Vaiṣnava*) [NS]: Sthanaka; the feet are kept 2½ talas apart, one foot sama, the other with toes pointing out and shank bent. Depicts persons of the superior and middling type.

VAIVARNYA (*Vaivarṇya*) [NS]: Change of colour; satvika bhava; vibhavas—cold, heat, anger, illness, hard work.

VAKSHASWASTIKA (*Vakṣaswastika*) [NS]: See *Karana.*

VALANA (*Valana*) [NS]: Uru krama, the knees are drawn inward and body is turned round.

VALITA (*Valita*) [NS]: Greeva bheda; the neck and face are turned sideways.

——— [NS]: See *Karana.*

——— [NS]: Nritta hasta; Lata hands are crossed at the elbow.

VALITORU (*Valitoru*) [NS]: See *Karana.*

VAMAVIDDHA (*Vāmaviddha*) [NS]: Akashiki mandala; the following charis are performed: right foot, Suchi, left Apakranta, right Dandapada, left Suchi, right Bhramari and Parshvakranta, left Akshipta, right Dandapada and Urudvritta, left Suchi, Bhramari and Alata, right Parshvakranta, left Atikranta.

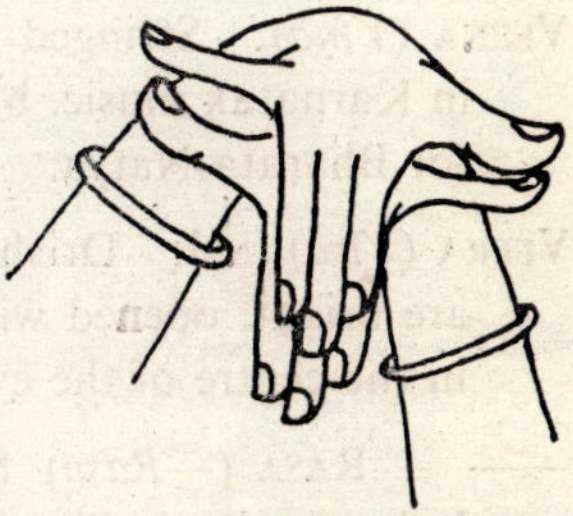

Varaha

VARAHA (*Varāha*) [AD]: Samyuta hasta; one Mrigashirsha hand is placed on the back of the other, the thumb of one meeting the little finger of the other and vice versa. Denotes a boar.

VARDHAMANA (*Vardhamāna*) [NS]: Samyuta hasta; a Mukula hand is grasped by Kapittha. Denotes grasping, receiving, persevering, convention, truthfulness, abridgement.

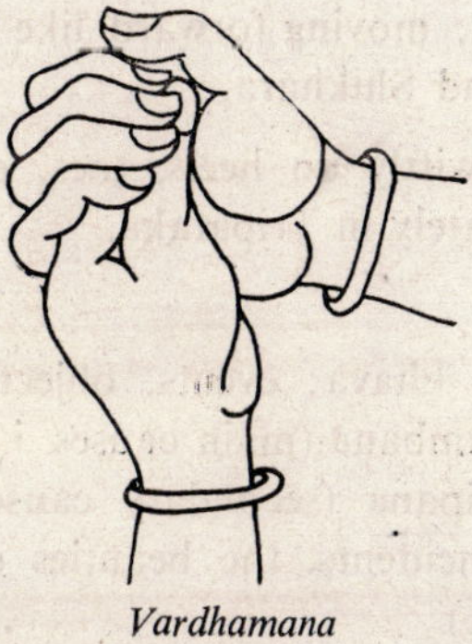

Vardhamana

VARNA (*Varṇa*): Piece de resistance of a Bharata Natya recital requiring skill in abhinaya, tala, and execution of adavu jatis. Pada varnas (see *Chauka-Varna*) are compositions in shringara rasa or in praise of a god or king and contain pallavi, anupallavi, chitteswara, charana, swara and swara-sahitya. Abhinaya performed to the singing of pallavi, anupallavi and sahitya of the chitteswara is alternated with increasingly complex and accelerated jatis, teermanams and adavus. Similarly for the charanas, swaras and swarasahityas. Also called Chauka-varna. Tana-varnas have more or less a similar structure, but the musical content of the raga rather than its sahitya is given prominence. Correspondingly the dancing emphasises nritta rather than abhinaya. May contain sahitya in shringara or bhakti rasa in praise of a god or a king. Sometimes called Swarajati or Swarajati varna.

VARTITA (*Varṭita*) [NS]: See *Karana*.

VASAKASAJJITA (*Vāsakasajjita*): A woman who adorns herself before meeting her lover. One of the ashta nayikas. See *Nayika*.

VEENA (*Vīṇā*): Stringed instrument; one of the most important in Karnatak music, but not used very much in accompaniment for Bharata Natya.

VEERA (*Vīra*) [NS]: Drishti bheda expressing veera rasa; the eyes are bright, opened wide, serious and agitated, the eyeballs are in the centre of the eyes.

———RASA (*—Rasa*) Sentiment of heroism; presiding deity—Indra; sthayi bhava—utsaha; representative colour—light orange. Vibhavas—presence of mind, perseverance, diplomacy, discipline, military strength, aggressiveness, reputation of might, etc.; anubhavas—firmness, patience, heroism, charity, diplomacy, etc.

———GATI (*—Gati*) [AD]: Gati bheda; moving forward like a hero with right hand Pataka, left hand Shikhara.

VEGINI (*Veginī*) [AD]: Chari; walking swiftly on heels, toes, or entire foot, holding each hand alternately in Tripataka.

VEPATU (*Vepatu*) [NS]: See *Kampa*.

VIBHAVA (*Vibhāva*): Determination of a bhava; events, objects, etc. giving rise to a bhava, may be alambana (main causes, i.e. nayaka-nayika relationship) or uddipana (secondary causes that further excite the bhava, e.g. incidents, the beauties of nature, encouragement of friends, etc.)

VIBODHA (*Vibodha*) [NS]: Vyabhichari bhava of awakening. Vibhavas—digestion of food, bad dreams, loud sounds, a touch etc; anubhavas—rubbing of the eyes, getting up, etc.

VIBHRANTA (*Vibhrānta*) [NS]: Confused; drishti bheda expressing vyabhichari bhava. The eyelids and eyeballs are moved and the middle of the eye is opened wide.

VICHITRA (*Vicitra*) [NS]: Akashiki mandala; the following charis are performed: right foot, Janita and Talasanchara chari, left Syandita and Bhujangatrasita, right Atikranta and Urudvritta, left Suchi, right Vikshipta, left Apakranta.

VICHYAVA (*Vicyava*) [NS]: Bhaumi chari, the feet are separated from Samapada and the forepart of each foot is struck on the ground.

VIDHUTA (*Vidhuta*) [NS]: Mukha bheda; the mouth is opened obliquely. Denotes restraining, saying 'not so' etc.

——— [NS]: Shiro bheda; the head is moved quickly from side to side. Denotes terror, panic, fever, cold, first stages of intoxication.

VIDYUDBHRANTA (*Vidyudbhrānta*) [NS]: See *Angahara*.

——— [NS]: Bhaumi chari; one foot is turned and touched to the back of the other foot and then stretched out, the head moving in a circle simultaneously.

——— [NS]: See *Karana*.

VIHASITA (*Vihāsita*): An aspect of hasya rasa; gentle laughter; a slight smile with soft laughter and cheerful face.

VIHRITA (*Vihrita*) [NS]: Akashiki mandala; the right foot is moved in Janita and Nikuttana charis, left Syandita, right Urudvritta, left Alata, right Suchi, left Parshvakranta, right Akshipta, Bhramari and Dandapada charis, left Suchi and Bhramari charis, right Bhujangatrasita and left Atikranta.

VIKOSHA (*Vikoṣa*) [NS]: Full blown; drishti bheda expressing vyabhichari bhava; the eyeballs are not steady and the eyelids are opened wide and held thus without blinking. Denotes joy.

VIKRISHTA (*Vikṛṣṭa*) [NS]: Nasika krama; the nostrils are blown out. Denotes a strange smell, breathing, anger, fear.

VIKSHIPTA (*Vikṣipta*) [NS]: See *Karana*.

VIKSHIPTAKSHIPTA (*Vikṣiptākṣipta*) [NS]: See *Karana*.

VIKUNITA (*Vikunita*) [NS]: Nasika krama; the nose is contracted or screwed up. Denotes laughter, disgust, envy.

VINIGUHANA (*Viniguhana*) [NS]: Adhara krama; the lips are drawn in and concealed. Denotes effort.

VINIVRITTA (*Vinivṛtta*) [NS]: See *Karana*.

——— [NS]: Mukha bheda; the mouth is spread out. Denotes jealousy, anger, contempt, envy in a woman.

VINIYOGA (*Viniyoga*): Usage.

VIOLIN (*Violin*): Stringed instrument used as an accompaniment for vocal music and dance.

VIPLUTA (*Vipluṭa*) [NS]: Disturbed; drishti bheda expressing vyabhichari bhava. The eyelids are trembled then held still with the eyeballs moving and disturbed.

VIPRALABDHA (*Vipralabdha*): A woman who has been deceived by her lover. One of the ashta nayikas. See *Nayika*.

VIPRAKIRNA (*Viprakīrṇa*) [NS]: See *Swastika*.

VIRAHOTKANTHITA (*Virahotkaṇṭhita*): A woman who is disturbed by the absence of her lover. One of the ashta nayikas. See *Nayika*.

VISARGA (*Visarga*) [NS]: Adhara krama; the lips are spread out. Denotes anger of woman, affected indifference, painting the lips.

VISHADA (*Viṣāḍa*) [NS]: Vyabhichari bhava of despair. Vibhavas —inability to finish work undertaken, accidents, calamities, etc.; anubhavas—(associated with persons of the superior and middling types)—seeking alms, thinking about means of livelihood, loss of energy, absent-mindedness, breathing deeply; (with persons of the inferior type)—running away, looking down, dryness of the mouth, licking the lips, breathing deeply, sleeping, meditating, etc.

VISHAMA (*Viṣama*) [AD]: Chari; walking forward with this movement—the left foot is set to the right of the right foot and then the right is set to the left of the left foot.

VISHANNA (*Viṣanna*) [NS]: Drishti bheda expressing vyabhichari bhava of Vishada or dejection. The eyes are bewildered, the eyelids drawn apart and held without blinking, with eyeballs motionless.

VISHKAMBHA (*Viṣkambha*) [NS]: See *Karana*.

——— [NS]: See *Angahara*.

VISHKAMBHAPASRITA (*Viṣkambhapasrita*) [NS]: See *Angahara*.

VISHNUDHARMOTTARA (*Viṣṇudharmottara*): Purana claiming Vishnu as the first exponent of dance. The story goes that having danced various angaharas, karanas and mandalas, Vishnu assumed the form of Hayagreeva and killed the demons Madhu and Kaitabha who had stolen the four Vedas. Vishnu then taught this dance to Brahma who in turn taught it to Shiva, who, mastering it, was then called Nataraja.

VISHNUKRANTA (*Viṣṇukrānta*) [NS]: See *Karana.*

VISMAYA (*Vismaya*) [NS]: Sthayi bhava of astonishment; gives rise to adbhuta rasa. Vibhavas—illusion, magic, greatness, extraordinary feats or skill in the arts; anubhavas—opening the eyes wide, moving the head, movements of the eyebrows.

VISMITA (*Vismita*) [NS]: Drishti bheda expressing vismaya, sthayi bhava of astonishment. The eyes are opened wide, eyeballs turned up and eyelids held motionless.

VITADITA (*Vitadita*) [NS]: Puta chalana; reflex action of closing the eyelids. Denotes sustaining an accidental injury.

VITARKA (*Vitarka*) [NS]: Vyabhichari bhava of deliberation. Vibhavas—doubt, thinking, perplexity, etc.; anubhavas—discussing, settling the point, concealment of the counsel etc.

VITARKITA (*Vitarkita*) [NS]: Conjecturing; drishti bheda expressing vyabhichari bhava of vitarka. The eyelids are turned up as in guessing, the eyeballs are fully blown and moved slowly.

VIVARTAKA (*Vivartaka*) [NS]: See *Karana.*

VIVARTANA (*Vivartana*) [NS]: Adhara krama; the lips are narrowed. Denotes envy, pain, contentment, laughter.

——— [NS]: Uru krama; turning round with heels drawn inward. Used in dance sequences to turn round quickly.

VIVARTITA (*Vivartiṭa*) [NS]: Parshva krama; the trika is turned round.

——— [NS]: Puta chalana; the eyelids are raised. Denotes anger.

VIVRITTA (*Vivṛtta*) [NS]: Greeva bheda; the neck and face are pushed forward. Denotes going towards one's own place.

——— [NS]: See *Karana.*

——— [NS]: Mukha bheda; the mouth is held open with the lips parted. Denotes laughter, sorrow, fear.

VRIDA (*Vṛda*): Vyabhichari bhava of shame. Vibhavas—humiliation, repentance etc.; anubhavas—covering the face, thinking with downcast face, drawing lines on the ground, touching one's clothes and rings, biting the nails etc.

VRISHABHAKRIDITA (*Vṛṣabhakrīḍita*) [NS]: See *Karana*.

VRISHCHIKA (*Vṛṣcika*) [NS]: See *Karana*.

VRISHCHIKANIKUTTITA (*Vṛṣcikanikuṭṭita*) [NS]: See *Karana*.

VRISHCHIKAPASRITA (*Vṛṣcikapasrita*) [NS]: See *Angahara*.

VRISCHIKARECHITA (*Vṛṣcikarecita*) [NS]: See *Karana*.

VRITTI (*Vṛtti*): Four styles of dancing, viz., arabhati (energetic, using veera and bibhatsa rasas), bharati (vachika or using words), kaishiki (graceful; using shringara and hasya rasas), sattvati (grand, devoid of pathos but using veera rasa).

VYABHICHARI BHAVA (*Vyabhicāri Bhāva*): Transitory states that carry or express sentiments; caused by vibhavas, expressed through anubhavas; 33 of these, viz. Alasya, Aṃarsha, Apasmara, Asuya, Autsukya, Avahitta, Avega, Chapalata, Chinta, Dainya, Dhriti, Garva, Glani, Harsha, Jadata, Mada, Marana, Mati, Moha, Nidra, Nirveda, Shanka, Shrama, Smriti, Supta, Trasa, Ugrata, Unmada, Vibhodha, Vishada, Vitarka, Vrida, Vyadhi. Also called Sanchari bhava.

VYADHI (*Vyādhi*) [NS]: Vyabhichari bhava of sickness. Vibhavas —derangement of the humours (vata, pittha, kapha); anubhavas—shivering, tremors, bending of the body, chattering of the teeth, narrowing of the nostrils, throwing off of the clothes, flinging hands and feet about, desire to roll on the ground, desire for coolness, lamentation, crying, etc.

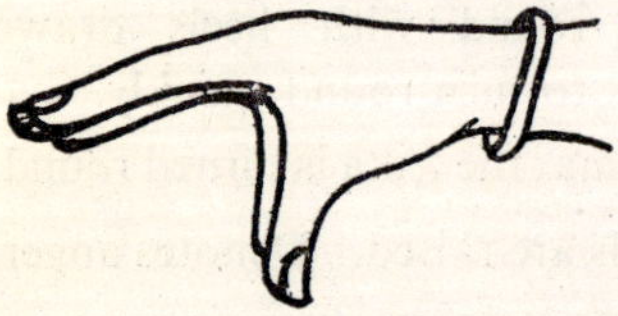
Vyaghra

VYAGHRA (*Vyāghra*) [AD]: One of the 4 extra asamyuta hastas; the thumb and little fingers of Mrigashirsha are bent down. Denotes tiger, monkey, frog, mother-of-pearl.

VYAMSITA (*Vyāmsita*) [NS]: See *Karana*.

VYANJANA (*Vyañjana*): The manner in which bhavas and rasa cause one another.

VYAVARTITA (*Vyāvartiṭa*) [NS]: Hasta karana; with the little finger, the fingers are gradually pointed inward and moved round.